THE UNLIKELY JOURNEY

DEREK STEWART

ISBN 978-0-615-58549-9

For Keisha, Coy, and Chayse

"Happy are those who dream dreams and are willing to pay the price to make them come true."-Anonymous

Acknowledgments

To my Lord and Savior, Jesus Christ. Thank you for...well, everything.

I would like to thank Keisha, Coy, and Chayse Stewart, my amazing family, for all of their love and support. It would have been impossible for me to complete this book with you. You all inspire me to be the best I can be every day.

To Brad and Keesha Sharp, your love, friendship, support, and encouraging words mean more than you'll ever know. I am honored and humbled to be called *friend* by the likes of you.

To Jaime Mendez and Essence Atkins for your hospitality, love, and support.

To all my friends and family who supported my vision for this book.

FORWARD

"All dreams come true....if we have the courage to pursue them."

I think a lot of us dream big when we are children. Early in life we have so much hope and faith, we truly believe we can do anything, even amidst the most dire circumstances. As we get older we learn that those dreams take work. Then because of life's many obstacles, we stop the pursuit.

However, not following your dreams is something that will haunt you and those around you for the rest of your life.

"I don't have time for dreams, I've got responsibilities"
"That dream wasn't meant for me, it was just that...a dream."

Right now, stop and think about those dreams of yours even if it's been awhile. Now, ask yourself - Why did you stop pursuing them?

"The Unlikely Journey" is the story of a family's road to success. About a Father who had dreams in his own life and no matter what others said, no matter the lack of ability, no matter the circumstances, he fought and achieved them. A Mother who, in spite of her fear, believed and had faith. And, because they listened and dedicated themselves to their son's dream, they discovered new dreams of their own. Yes, our dreams can change. What a beautiful thing. No one is limited in the amount of dreams they have. The only thing that limits us is *us*.

They are the Stewarts. And their story will give you the strength to give your dreams the dedication and hard work they deserve.

Who are the Stewarts?

Meeting them you can't help but feel the sense of unity. Such a beautiful family inside and out. I remember the first time I met them. It was our first table read for "Are We There Yet?". I was sitting at the table watching all the other actors come to their seats. I remember seeing this cute little boy sit in his assigned seat. "Oh he's playing Kevin" I thought to myself. Mr. Ali Leroi (director, producer) had us all introduce ourselves before we began, and then it was time to start.

As we began, Coy shined. I remember thinking, "Wow, this little boy is really good, so natural." And I wasn't the only one. We were all blown away by his abilities and of course when we were done, I wanted to find his parents!! They needed to know how gifted he was, just in case they didn't know.

When I approached Coy and looked up at his 6'7" father, Derek, I let him know my feelings. They were both so kind and humble. Coy proceeded to tell me that his mom's name was Keisha (one letter different than mine) and that she was a huge fan. I met 5'3 Keisha Stewart (yes 5'3 don't let her fool you) later that day with Coy's little brother Chayse happily tagging along. Instantly, Keisha and I connected as if we had known each other for years.

Over the course of the next year and a half we became very close. We consider the Stewarts family.

Derek Stewart is a man who doesn't make "to do lists", he just does. Although he is known for his great accomplishments in basketball, he has a new, even greater gift as a writer, balancing eloquence and honesty. And in the pages that follow you will discover that.

"The Unlikely Journey" is a testimony about faith. A journey to put your trust in God and watch how He provides.

My hope is that you read this story and decide to have the courage to boldly pursue your dreams. God Bless you in your own journey.

Keesha Sharp

CONTENTS

INTRODUCTION

Have you ever looked at your life and asked yourself, "How did I get here?" Whether you were at a good place, or a place that you didn't want to be, you had to take a minute to trace the steps that led you to that point. And "here" is not necessarily a physical place, although often times it is. "Here" could also be a certain time in your life. I had one of those moments back in August of 2010. For me, it was both the physical place AND that particular time in my life. It was a scorching summer day and I was sitting on a bench right outside of Jackie Robinson Park on the corner of Bradhurst Ave. and 154th in Harlem, New York. My exact location holds significance because, well, my home is Columbia, South Carolina. How I got there is an interesting story. What I was doing, even more so.

Before I get into the story, I feel it necessary to give a little background on my family. I met my wife, Keisha, in 1991 while we were both students at Augusta College (now Augusta State University) in Augusta, Ga. She was a freshman who transferred in from Norfolk State during the spring of my sophomore year. We met through mutual friends and started dating in the fall of that year. It wasn't long after that that I realized that she was the one. I know that I was young at the time but there was something about her that gave me a level of comfort that I had never felt before. We had come from two different worlds but shared something that connected us on the deepest of levels.

Keisha lost her mother when she was 7 and went to live with her father and older half sisters. Having lived with her mother her entire life, she never really felt like she belonged once she moved in with them. She had a close relationship with her father but her relationship with her sisters was strained at best. She never really connected with that side of her family and as a result, as soon as she graduated from high school, she left for college at Norfolk State University in Virginia. After a semester, she decided to transfer to Augusta College in Augusta, GA and briefly moved in with some family members on her mother's side that lived there. While her relationship with them was better, she still never really fit in there either because she didn't grow up with them. All of this left her with a huge void in her life.

I grew up with my mother and stepfather. I always knew about my biological father but never really had him in my life until my teenager years. Even then it was sparingly. I would describe my childhood this way: not as bad as other people have experienced, not as good as I would have liked. I have an older sister with whom I was never really close. My brother is 5 years younger than me. He and I have always been really close and continue to be to this day. In addition, I have two younger siblings on my father's side. I am much older than they are and having grown up in different households, am not particularly close to them either. Our parents provided food, clothing, and shelter and I never doubted that they loved me. But having a mean, alcoholic stepfather didn't foster a very supportive, nurturing household. At times, I felt like I didn't belong. Like I wasn't supposed to be there, I was supposed to be with my biological father. But then I would realize that I didn't really know him, so I didn't belong there either.

I had dreams of creating a better life for myself after Igraduated from high school. I fell in love with the game of basketball at an early age and that was going to be my ticket. I started playing competitively in junior high and made the junior varsity my freshman year. My parents never really supported me in this. They didn't discourage me from playing, they just didn't support me. In four years of playing through high school, they attended one game. One. And that was the last home game of my senior year. My coached called and asked them to come. Throughout my entire high school career, I had to find my own way to and from practice and games. During the summers, it was completely up to me to raise the money I needed in order to be able to attend the team basketball camps that we would go to every year. To say that I was completely on my own when it came to my basketball dreams is no exaggeration.

My mother was in the military. During my high school years, we lived in Ft. Stewart, GA. At the beginning of my junior year, she left to begin a tour of duty in Korea. My brother and I were left in the care of my stepfather. There is a popular Temptations song that always reminds me of him and our life during that time: *Papa Was a Rollin' Stone*. Over the next year and a half, it was nothing for him to leave home on a Thursday or Friday night, and not be seen again until Monday or Tuesday. So during my junior and senior year, I basically raised my younger brother while going to school, working here and there, and playing basketball.

So like Keisha, when I graduated, I ran for the hills! I had earned a full athletic scholarship to play basketball at Augusta College. After a solid four year career, I jumped at an opportunity to play professionally in Germany. Keisha came with me and we were married in December of 1993 in Wurzburg, GE. We would spend the next eight plus years living in France, Germany, and Israel as that opportunity turned into a nine year career. Our oldest son, Tyson Coy Stewart, was born on June 24, 1998. He was truly a blessing. We had lost two babies in the first trimester over the years and were starting to think that kids might not be in the cards for us. Born 7 weeks premature, he weighted only 3lbs 12oz but had no major health issues. We felt very fortunate. He had to stay in the NICU for two weeks before we were able to bring him home. We were thankful and pledged to be the kind of parents that we always wanted our parents to be. Two weeks after Coy came home, I had to leave for France. I had signed to play for a team there a couple of months prior and it was time for me to report to training camp. Leaving them was the hardest thing that I've ever had to do. Fortunately, Coy was well enough to travel a couple of months later and they were able to join me.

A couple of years later, I signed to play in Israel for the second time. Keisha and I wanted Coy to be closer to home so that he could spend time with family, her father in particular, so we decided that they would stay. It was a difficult season for me to say the least. I saw them once for four days during that ten month span. When I returned home at the end of that season, Keisha and Coy came to pick me up from the airport. They were waiting for me at the gate (this was pre-9-11 days) and Coy was in her arms. I approached them and reached out for him, waiting to see if he would want to come to me. He gave me a look that said, "You look familiar...but I don't know." Broke...my...heart. He was about to turn three and I realized that I had missed almost an entire year of his life that I would never get back.

Although I would wrestle with the idea of retiring for the rest of the summer, the decision, I suspect, was made at that moment at the airport. By the time September rolled around, and it was getting close to my departure time, the terrible tragedy that came to be known simply as 9-11 changed things for me, (and everyone else for that matter) forever. Having made countless transatlantic flights since 1993 because of my career without a second thought of anything ever happening to me, the tragic events of that day made me realize how fortunate I truly was. It was time for me to appreciate the time I had playing the game I loved for as long as I had played, and get to the business of family.

So in September of 2001 at the age of 30, I retired and we settled in Keisha's hometown of Columbia, SC. I got a job working at a mortgage company and two years later, we purchased our first home. We settled in and started living "the American Dream". Working at the mortgage company satisfied me for a while because it was so different from what I had been doing for the previous nine years. But it wasn't long before I was missing the game. To satisfy my basketball jones, I left the mortgage company in 2004 to coach at a local high school. This lasted for a couple of years before I realized that high school was not the place for me. God bless all the amazing teachers educating our kids but lesson plans and parent/teacher conferences are not my idea of a good time. Plus, I became frustrated with the stifling rules on the amount of time I could spend working with my players. I didn't want to deal with all of that. I just wanted to teach the game of basketball to kids who wanted to learn and show them how the discipline and dedication that goes into being a successful athlete, could help them be successful at anything they wanted to do. With that in mind I left the high school and started a basketball training company designed to provide people of all ages and skill level with the necessary tools to be successful. Shortly after that on August 31, 2006, we were blessed with our second child, Peyton Chayse Stewart. Our little family was complete.

A couple of years later, the economy tanked and things got a little hairy financially, but all in all, we were happy. We had two beautiful, healthy boys and took great joy in creating the kind of atmosphere in our family that fostered love, encouragement, and support for one another. It's something neither of us had during our childhood which is the link between us. Because we both understood what that felt like, we were able to fill that void in each other's lives. It's why we work so well together and why we raise our kids the way we do.

During Coy's early years, people began noticing things about him that we kind of took for granted. He was very smart, articulate, and mature for a kid his age. I can't count the number of times complete strangers would compliment us on his behavior, vocabulary, and personality. He would say things that most 3 and 4 year olds don't normally say but because he was our first child, we didn't think anything of it. We thought that all kids his age were like that. Now Chayse is the same way. Very smart and articulate for his age with a very distinct personality. A friend of mine likes to say of both of them that they've "been here before".

Our goal for them from day one was to prepare them to be successful. We want them to be in a position, as they get older, to achieve anything they want. While there is nothing wrong with being mediocre, we want them to be more. We want them to know that there are no limitations and they don't have to settle in life. To that end, we always encourage them to believe that. I can remember when Coy was 3 and 4 years old. Keisha would be in the kitchen cooking and he would be riding his tricycle around in a circle just hanging out with her. She would tell him to repeat after her.

"I. Can. Do. Anything!"

"I. Am. Smart!"

"I. Am. Amazing!"

Where she got that from, I have no idea. But I thought it was a wonderful way of reinforcing how we wanted him to feel about himself. As he got older, it became clear to us that Coy was even more special than we thought. We truly believed that he was destined for greatness. This is the story of how that greatness manifested itself. The story of how allowing him to follow his dreams jump started a journey and changed the course of our lives. Forever. It is a story of love, family, sacrifice, and faith. I hope you enjoy the ride. We certainly are.

1

THE

BEGINNING

At the end of Coy's fourth grade year at Lake Carolina Elementary , he informed us that he didn't want to play sports that summer like he normally did. We asked what he wanted to do and he said that he didn't know. Just something different. Keisha had become friends with the mother of one of Coys' classmates at the time. Ericka Deabreu is a former model and owner of DeAbreu Modeling and Consulting in Columbia. She told Keisha that she had acting classes for kids and that the summer session was about to start. Maybe Coy would like to do that. We asked Coy if he was interested and he said yes so we took him to a class. After it was over, we asked if he liked it. The answer was an emphatic yes! He really had a lot of fun and asked us if he could go again. We of course said yes. We were just happy that he found something that he could do for the summer, be introduced to something new, and have fun.

About three weeks after he started taking classes, Ericka got a few of the people in her program on as extras [1]in a movie that was being filmed in Columbia. *Nailed* is a film starring Jessica Biel, Jake Gyllenhaal, and Tracy Morgan about a woman who gets a nail lodged in her head and ends up in Washington lobbying for better health care. Coy and I were the father and son in a family of four that was supposed to be vacationing in DC. We were told to bring in four different "vacation" outfits apiece for the wardrobe department to choose from for us to wear in the scene that we would be in.

---

[1] *Extras- Actors on movie or tv sets with non-speaking roles who are usually designated to the background.*

We got to the shoot location downtown promptly at 7 am. The South Carolina State House was doubling as our nation's capital. We were directed by a production assistant (PA) [2]to a huge tent designated as holding[3]. It was filled with about 30 other extras. After waiting around for about an hour, another PA came and got 20 of us and led us to the wardrobe trailer. Once there, the people in the wardrobe department went through our outfits and picked out something for us to wear. From there, we were taken to a set of smaller tents where we changed. Then it was back to holding where we sat for another hour.

Finally, another PA came and led the group to the set, which on this day was the back of the State House. Coy and I were paired with a woman and little girl to make up the vacationing family. Our instructions were to walk down the steps of the State House and head to the right once we got to the bottom. We would be a part of the background while they filmed a scene between Jessica and Tracy. The scene took approximately two

[2] *Production Assistant (PA)- Workers on a movie or tv set that are tasked with a wide range of responsibilities critical to the success of a production.*
[3] *Holding- An area on a movie or tv set designated for extras while they are waiting for their scene.*

hours to shoot. We had to do it over, and over, and over again.

Between each take[4], we stood around for 10-15 minutes while

they figured out...whatever it is they were trying to figure out.

Meanwhile, it was getting closer to noon and the temperature

was steady rising. Let's not forget that it was June. In South

Carolina.

As it got hotter, they started having PA's stand next to Jessica

and Tracy holding umbrella's over their heads to shield them

from the sun. I thought that this was a good learning

opportunity for Coy and pointed it out to him. Keisha and I have

always taught him that no one is better than anyone else. That

he should treat all people the same, no matter who they are.

Well clearly, those moral lines are sometimes blurred. Especially

in this industry. I told him that these two actors may be more

important than the rest of us to this movie production, but that

doesn't make them better people than us.

After they were done with the scene, we were taken to yet

---

[4] *Take- Each time a scene is filmed.*

another tent for lunch. It was a buffet and we ate with the other

extras and the crew[5]. Once lunch was over, we were taken to

the courtyard behind the state house to shoot another scene.

This time, we were instructed to start at one place and walk in a

particular direction, again providing background for a scene

with Jessica and Tracy. This lasted for another two hours. During

lunch, I had prepared myself mentally for the standing around.

But the heat was another story. Again, it was June. In South

Carolina. After about 15 takes, they were finally done. We went

back to the wardrobe trailer and got the other clothes that we

had brought. There was some paperwork to fill out and sign and

then we were free to go.

All in all, it was an interesting, fun day. I've always loved movies

and enjoy watching behind the scene clips. This was that to the

10th power. I had no idea before that day how much went into

making a film. It is a long, arduous process. I can't say that I left

feeling like, "Man, I want to be an actor!" It was more like,

---

[5] *Crew- The various employees, with the exception of the actors, on a movie or tv set. This includes, but is not limited to, camera operators, electricians, set designers, etc.*

"Man, I don't see how they do this!" Coy on the other hand, had a blast. He was so excited when we left. He enjoyed the whole experience and was especially happy that he got a chance to interact with the two main actors. During a break in the first scene, Tracy Morgan was sitting in a chair about 20 feet from us. Coy wanted to meet him but was afraid that he might be mean. I explained to him that Tracy had kids of his own so I doubted that he would be mean to another kid. Getting up his courage, Coy approached Tracy, stuck his hand out and said, "Hi Mr. Morgan, my name is Coy. It's an honor to be on set with you." Tracy shook his hand and said, "Cool beans man." Later, while shooting the second scene, he spoke to Jessica Biel between shots. She was walking by headed back to her mark[6] and he said, "Hi Ms Biel." She turned around, saw him, gave him a huge smile, waved and said, "Hi cutie." Those two exchanges, along with being on set and seeing how everything worked made it a positive experience for him. On the way home, Coy was sitting in the backseat, staring out of the window.

---

[6] *Mark- Placements on the floor or ground where actors are required to stand during particular scenes.*

"Dad."

"Yeah."

"I know what I want to do."

"Do about what?"

"No...I mean I know what I want to be."

"Oh. What do you want to be?"

"I want to be an actor."

"Really?! Even after standing around all day in the sun like that?"

"I don't care. I loved it. That's what I want to do."

"Ok."

Now up to this point, he had never said anything about wanting to act. He was going to class every week and having fun but had never said anything about actually wanting to be an actor. I was looking at him through the rearview mirror the whole time. He was completely lost in thought. I know my son and I had never seen that look on his face before. But I knew it well. It was a familiar look because it was the look that a person has when they fall in love with something or someone. Their mind overflowing with thoughts of being with that person. Or doing

that thing that makes them so happy.

When we got home, he told my wife all about everything we

had done that day and how much fun he'd had. He also told her

the same thing he told me in the car. He said that he wanted to

be an actor on television and in the movies. That night, she and

I discussed it and quickly came to the decision that we would do

whatever we had to do to support him if he was serious. This

goes back to our respective childhoods. Supporting him was a

no-brainer for us because it was something that we didn't get

from our parents. From a young age, we introduced Coy to

various things. Basketball, soccer, baseball, football, tap dance,

golf, drums. We encouraged him to get involved with extra-

curricular activities at school like student council, video club,

etc. Anything that would stimulate his mind and broaden his

interests, we were all for.

The next day we sat him down and had a discussion with him.

We told him that we would support him and do anything we

could to help him achieve his goal but that we would only take it as serious as he does. He would have to make sure that he maintained his A/B average in school, went to every acting class that he was suppose to, and worked hard at being the best he could be. We also talked to him about how difficult it was to achieve success in that particular field. Nothing is ever guaranteed but if he worked hard and dedicated himself to it, he could eventually be as successful as he wanted. He looked us straight in the eye and said, "Ok."

A couple of days later, Keisha called me from work and said that she had just gotten off the phone with Ericka. She had asked Keisha if she thought I would be interested in auditioning for a commercial. *Me??A commercial?? Really??* Apparently, they were looking for basketball players for this particular spot and she knew that I was a former player. The way it works is like this: Ericka is what you would call a "Mother Agent". [7]She recruits and prepares talent to work in larger markets so she

---

[7] *Mother Agent-A talent agency that finds talent in small markets cities and prepares them for introduction to agencies in bigger markets.*

has contacts in places like Atlanta, GA, and Charlotte and

Greensboro, NC. Because of this, she receives audition notices

for projects being filmed in these markets. She also has contacts

in places like Los Angeles and New York and can refer her talent

to agents in these markets.

I called Ericka to get some more information about the audition.

She told me that they were casting for a commercial with

someone named...

"Coach K? Have you ever heard of a Coach K??"

" Uhh...yeah Ericka, I've heard of him."

For those of you who may not know, Coach K is the nickname of

Hall of Fame Duke University men's basketball coach, Mike

Krzyzewski. The audition was in the next day in Raleigh, NC.

There were no lines to learn. All I had to do was make any kind

of basketball move and then finish with a dunk. I told Ericka,

"I think I can do that."

Before heading to the audition, I had to get a headshot[8] for

Ericka to submit. So that evening, her assistant took a picture of

me standing up against the wall outside of her studio. I printed

a couple of copies out at Walgreens and the next day, gassed up

the SUV and headed to Raleigh. During the drive, I thought

about how just three days ago, I had spent an entire day on a

movie set, thanking God that I didn't have to make a living doing

it. Now here I was driving 2 ½ hours each way for the

opportunity to do just that! The fact is, Coach K being involved

made the decision easy. As a former player and current fan of

the game, meeting him and having a chance to pick his brain

was well worth a day of standing around on a commercial set.

But I also thought about how deciding to help Coy pursue his

dreams had all of a sudden opened the doors to a whole new

world for myself and possibly Keisha and Chayse. I wondered

what else it would bring in the months and possibly years to

come.

---

[8] *Headshot-A picture used by actors and models when attempting to get work.*

I followed the navigational directions and ended up in a residential neighborhood. Seeing as how the audition consisted of making basketball moves and dunking, I assumed that the location would be at a gym. Which meant that I was lost. I decided to continue to follow the directions anyway and ended up at a house. There were several cars parked in front of the house and I could see a small crowd of people near the garage so I thought maybe this could be the place. I parked and headed up the driveway towards the house. The driveway was on a slight hill and as I got to the top of the hill, I saw a basketball goal, a camera, and a bunch of guys who looked like basketball players milling around. This was the place. I guess my expectations were too high to assume that the audition would actually take place in a gym.

There was a table set up with two ladies signing people in. I went and introduced myself and signed in. There were guys already going through the audition so I watched a few while I changed my shoes. They were looking to cast 10 guys and based on what I had seen so far, I felt like I had a pretty good chance.

Don't get me wrong. I'm not arrogant or anything. But I played basketball on just about every level for most of my life. I know what I can and can't do. I stretched a little bit and then it was my turn. I walked out to the guy who was directing everyone. He was a relatively nice guy and told me that all he needed was a simple basketball move and a dunk. It wasn't until that moment that I decided what I was going to do. I grabbed a basketball and walked towards the right side of what would have been the free throw line on a real court. The plan was to keep it simple. I dribbled to my right a couple of times, changed directions with a behind the back dribble to my left, took one more dribble towards the basket with my left hand, and then jumped. When I planted to jump, I made every effort to jump as high as I could. This was very important because although I was still playing pickup basketball a couple of times a week, at 37 years old, I was no spring chicken, as they say. It had been quite some time since I had jumped high enough to dunk and the last thing I wanted to do was get stuck on the rim.

As I rose up towards the basket, the rim was getting closer a lot faster than it should have been. Now, during my playing days, I was known for my jumping ability. But I had no problem accepting the fact that my high jumping days were behind me. Still, this rim is getting closer, and closer. Then it hit me. Regulation basketball goals are 10 feet high. That's what I'm accustomed to dunking on so I jumped based on that fact. This goal, having been set up in someone's driveway and all, was only at about 9 feet. Meaning that I would clear the basket with room to spare.

When I realized this, I decided to showboat a little and brought the ball all the way behind my head, touching the back of my neck, before throwing it through. On the way down, I heard a bunch of "Ooh's" and "Aaah's" so I figured it went over well. The director shook my hand and told me that it was the best one so far. Having done my thing, I got back into my SUV, and headed back to Columbia. I thought about how funny it was that I had traveled 5 hours round trip to an audition that lasted only ten minutes!! The life of an actor. How do they do it?

Ericka called me the next day and told me that I got the job. I was excited! More so about meeting Coach K than about being in the commercial. A couple of days later, I left Columbia at 3am headed back to Raleigh. I had to be at a hotel there at six to meet the other nine guys who had been cast. We all loaded into two 15 passenger vans and were taken to the Duke University basketball practice facility in Durham. Once there, we met the director who would be shooting the spot. He gave us a little background on himself and then explained what we would be doing. The spot was for a company that made artificial hips. Having had hip replacement surgery, Coach K was endorsing their product. They would basically be filming us as he took us through some light basketball drills, as if conducting a practice, proving that one could maintain mobility after having hip replacement surgery using this company's artificial hip.

We divided ourselves into two groups of five and put on the practice uniforms they had provided for us. The day was very much like it was on the set of *Nailed.* A lot of takes and a lot of standing around and waiting. The problem this time was that every time we stood around for 10-15 minutes, it would take us another 10-15 minutes to get warmed up again. The good thing was that while we were standing around, we had a chance to talk with Coach K. He was really nice and open and it was a cool experience to be able to talk with a legend of the game.

At 2 o'clock, after multiple takes of multiple drills from multiple angles, we were finally done. I filled out all of my paperwork so that I could get paid my $188.00 after taxes, and headed home. On my way back, I was thinking about the day, and it hit me: *How did I get here?? How did I go from regular, everyday life, to being on a movie set and shooting a commercial in the same week??* It's funny how quickly it happened after Coy said that he wanted to be an actor. But little did I know, it was only a preview of what was coming.

In July, Ericka Deabreu brought in an acting coach from LA to do a three day boot camp with her students. Patrick Malone is an 18 year acting veteran/coach who owns The Actor's Spot acting studio in North Hollywood. He came in and taught the kids various things like auditioning techniques, acting for the camera, commercial scenes, film scenes, monologues, etc. It was really a great experience for them to learn from someone who has been doing it for such a long time. On the last day of the session, the parents were invited to come and watch our kids do a commercial and film scene. It was our first time seeing Coy act. Deabreu didn't allow the parents to watch the classes for fear that some of the kids wouldn't be as focused as they needed to be. Keisha and I were pleasantly surprised. He seemed very comfortable and natural.

Once they were all done, we (meaning the parents) had the opportunity to speak with Patrick individually and get feedback on our kids. He told us that Coy was a very talented actor. He said that he was a natural and had all the tools to make it in the business. We were happy to hear that but didn't put much stock in it at the time because, what did that really mean? Did it mean he's going to make it? Did it mean he was going to be this big star? No. It didn't. It meant that an acting coach from LA thought that he was good. When he returned to LA, Patrick called Ericka and told her basically the same thing "You've got some pretty good kids, but that Stewart kid is the one! He is a natural and has all the tools to be successful in the business." He also told his wife about Coy...but we'll get to that later.

2

THE JOURNEY BEGINS

Things were pretty quiet the rest of the summer. Coy continued

taking classes once a week and was still having fun. In July, the

kids at DeAbreu began preparing for the Talent Extravaganza

that she has a couple of times a year. This extravaganza is great

for two reasons. One: it's an opportunity for them to showcase

their skills and talents in front of friends and family. Two: there

would also be a few talents agents from larger markets there as

well. They would be judging the competition and looking for

talent to represent. The competition consisted of modeling and

acting. There were three different outfits that they would model

and each child was given a monologue, commercial scene, or

film scene to perform.

Coy was really excited about it, which made us excited. While he worked on his scene every week in class, Keisha was busy looking for outfits for him to wear. This was right up her alley because she loves to shop and has always done a great job of dressing the boys anyway. As for me, there wasn't really much I could do to help. Normally, I would have been working with him every day, helping him get ready. But I'm not an actor so there wasn't really much I could do. I just encouraged him and told him to be focused during his classes so that he would be prepared to do his best when the time came.

After a couple of months of preparation, the time for the extravaganza had finally arrived. The event was on a Sunday afternoon in one of the ballrooms at the Embassy Suites. I arrived an hour before our scheduled time so that I could attend a Q&A session with one of the agents. Heather Finn is a talent agent from Frontier Booking International in New York. She was one of the judges and was kind enough to take some time out and talk to the parents about the industry. She gave us some really good information about what's expected of kids and parents, what talent agents look for, what casting directors look for, etc. It was very interesting and informative. Once the competition started, Keisha was in the back with Coy to help him change outfits while I sat in the audience with Chayse. There was a really good turnout. About 200 people showed up to support the participants. This was great but added to my already anxious disposition.

The show started with all of the competitors walking the catwalk in small groups until they were all on stage together. The modeling competition was first. There were three different categories so this took about an hour and a half to get through. The acting competition was next. Each child had a contestant number pinned to their shirt, which allowed the agents to identify them. As they went through and the kids came out and did their monologues and film scenes, I was impressed. I thought that they all did a good job. As far as I was concerned, anyone who had the guts to get on stage and perform in front of a crowd of people were winners anyway. Especially kids!

The closer they got to calling Coy's number, the more nervous I got. This was new territory for me because I didn't really have a hand in preparing him for what he was about to do so I had no idea how it was going to be. Preparation has always been an important part of my life. I learned at an early age that preparation breeds confidence. Confidence breeds success. Think about it. When you were in school and you had a test to take, if you had studied for that test like you were suppose to, you walked into the classroom feeling confident about how you were going to do. But if you hadn't studied, if you waited until the last minute and tried to cram, you went in feeling worried and uneasy, with no confidence. As a player, I always worked extremely hard in every off season preparing myself for the season. This preparation led to me being confident in what I was going to be able to do. This confidence was key in my success. I always used the same approach with Coy. Whether it was when he played basketball, football, baseball, or soccer. Or if he was preparing for a vocabulary test in school. I always worked with him. Preparing him. Giving him, and myself, the confidence he needed to be successful. This was different. I was out of my element so there wasn't much that I could do.

Over the couple of months leading up to the show, Coy had performed his commercial scene for us several times. I thought he was good, but what did I know? Plus, doing it at home in front of us was completely different than doing it on a stage in front of 200 strangers. As it got closer to the time for him to go on, I had all kinds of crazy thoughts going through my mind...

"What if he gets nervous??"

"What if he forgets his lines??"

"What if they boo him??"

When he came out and started doing his thing, he put all of my fears to rest. It was as if he'd been doing it his entire life. When he was done, he got the loudest applause I'd heard up to that point. He ended up winning first place in the acting category and finishing in second place in two other categories. Insane!! Who knew?? When it was over, there were callbacks[9] for the agents that were there. This is where they meet the parents and

---

[9] *Callback- When after an initial audition, the casting director, director, or agent wants to see the actor again for a follow up.*

the child and express interest in possibly working with them.

Coy got callbacks from Heather Finn of Frontier Booking, as well

as two other agents from North Carolina. One was from

Greensboro and the other, Scott Cooper, was the owner of

Wilhelmina Evolution in Charlotte. This was an exciting time for

all of us because we had no idea that Coy was that talented. I

remember getting home that night and feeling like I had just

gotten drafted in the first round of the NBA draft. We were all

just so excited that he had done so well. In talking to the agents,

my wife and I felt like maybe he could end up doing a few local

or regional commercials or something. Little did we know, this

was just the beginning...

After discussing our options with Ericka, we decided to go with

the agency located in Greenville, NC. Apparently, you can have

multiple agents as long as they aren't in the same market.

Therefore, we had to choose between this agency and

Wilhelmina Evolution. The decision was more difficult than one

might think. We really liked Scott Cooper and felt like he was

sincere in his kind words about Coy. But after researching both agencies extensively, it was obvious that his agency was VERY successful. They had launched the careers of Brooklyn Decker and Jessica Stroup among others. With Coy just starting out, we didn't want him to get lost in the shuffle. So at the time, the Greenville agency seemed like our best bet.

They sent us a bunch of paperwork to fill out so that they could have a file on Coy. Basic info such as a detailed physical description, headshot, specific skills, etc. They said that they would start submitting him for jobs in the North Carolina market. They explained to us that since we weren't anywhere near Hollywood, jobs consisted primarily of print ads (magazine or newspaper advertisements) and local or regional commercials, with the occasional national commercial or small part as an extra in a film. While we were all excited about the possibilities, things kind of went back to normal. We didn't just sit around waiting for the phone to ring. Coy continued taking classes at Deabreu, having fun and getting better each week. Keisha and I sort of just got back into our daily routine.

Time slowly passed by without a phone call from our new talent agency. We asked Ericka if it was normal not to hear from your agent for weeks at a time. She said that it's like that sometimes but that it was ok for us to call them just to check in and keep Coy fresh in their minds. So I did. I called and left a message for the agent that we had met and signed with. A few days went by without a return call, so I called again. And again. And again. Finally, I called Ericka again and told her that I hadn't received a return call from them after several phone calls. I expressed our feeling that maybe we had made a mistake. Maybe we would have been better off with the agency in Charlotte. Ericka said that she would call and see what was going on. So she did. Ten minutes after my conversation with her, I got a call from the agent. She gave me a few apologetic words, said that they were really busy, but nothing had come up for Coy yet and she would be in touch next week. Of course next week came and went with no phone call.

This is where my experience as a pro basketball player came into play. I discovered very quickly that dealing with entertainment agents was no different than dealing with sports agents. The first thing to understand is that they only get paid if you get paid. For some agents, this means that they will ALWAYS give more attention to the clients who book the most jobs and therefore, bring in the most money. These are the clients whose phone calls get returned within the hour. Some of these agents will sign as many clients as they can, sort of a "throw it all against the wall and see what sticks" type of mentality. It's not personal and it doesn't necessarily mean that these kinds of agents are bad people. It's just the way they operate. Fortunately, all agents don't operate that way. There are some who genuinely care about the people they represent. They sign people they truly feel have a chance to be successful and then do all they can to help them achieve that success. Their clients are treated as people, not as dollar signs. The trick is trying to figure out which kind you're dealing with as quickly as possible. In the beginning, they all sound pretty much the same. But just like anything else in life, if something doesn't sound or feel right, it probably isn't.

Now, the fact that Coy hadn't been called for an audition three months after we signed with them, meant one of two things: 1). There hadn't been any parts for him to audition for...or 2). They were busy servicing their clients who were already working consistently. My experience led me to believe that it was probably a combination of both, with number 2 being the main reason. Why? Because even if no parts for Coy had come across their desk, they still would have returned my phone calls so that they could say, "Sorry Mr. Stewart but there haven't been any parts for Coy to audition for recently." The fact that they didn't even do that simply means that he was at the very bottom of the totem pole and at that time, wasn't important enough to spend time on. Again, nothing personal.

Keisha and I talked about the situation and informed Ericka that we thought it best to end our agreement with them and give Wilhelmina Evolution a try. If they would still have us. She made a phone call to them and they were excited to welcome us to their agency. Ericka dictated a letter that I typed up and sent to the Greenville agency, ending our contract with them effective in 30 days. This is one of the good things about signing with an agency. You can always get out if you feel you've made a mistake. (Also, know that it goes both ways) We weren't upset with the Greenville agency at all. We understood that it was a business. We just felt like there was no point in having an agent just for the sake of saying that you have an agent. The point was to try and get Coy opportunities to do what he loved to do.

3

BEST OVERALL

Things were better with Wilhelmina. Although they didn't send

Coy out on any auditions either, the communication was much

better. We at least felt like they had Coy on their minds. Scott

was great. He really liked Coy from the moment he saw him at

the DeAbreu Extravaganza. What really stuck out about him for

Keisha and me was that when we met with him during the

callback, he not only spoke about Coy's talent, but he

mentioned that Coy seemed like a really good kid and it was

important to him to work with good people. He had also invited

Coy to participate in his Talent, Inc. Showcase while we were

still with the agency in Greensboro. Which, to me, spoke

volumes about the kind of person he was and how much he

thought of Coy. The Showcase is held in March in Orlando every year and features talent from all over the southeast. There were several other students from DeAbreu invited as well. This is where things started to get interesting for us.

At that time, we were basically a one income family. My wife was a supervisor at a wireless company and was the primary breadwinner in our family. My basketball training company's services fell under the category of "disposable income" and when the bottom fell out of the economy in 2008, disposable income was something that a lot of people no longer had. I lost over 80% of my clients and our household income suffered as a result. I had also returned to school to finish my bachelor's degree. Between the end of 2007 and fall of 2009, I worked at Lowe's, Sam's Club, and UPS at various times in addition to trying to keep Jumpball Training afloat AND attend school four nights a week .The cost of attending Scott Cooper's Talent Inc. showcase was approximately $1,900.00. This included several acting and modeling workshops that were to be conducted by various agents who had been working in the industry for some time, three acting competitions, a special talent competition (i.e. Dance, singing, instrument), and the modeling competition. Also, just like at DeAbreu's Extravaganza, there would be a callback session, giving the kids the opportunity to meet with the agents who were interested in representing them. It did not include, however, transportation, food, and lodging. Needless to say, we couldn't afford to take Coy AND pay all of our bills on time. This is where our belief that it was our duty as parents to support our kids' dreams came into play. I would say that Keisha and I discussed what we were going to do, but that would be a lie. The truth is, there was no discussion. After Coy said that he really wanted to go, our conversation went something like this...

"So what are we going to do?" she asked.

"What do you mean? We're going to take him. How can we not?" I replied.

"Ok. I just wanted to make sure we were on the same page." She said.

So that pretty much set the tone for how we were going to handle the financial situation at that point and going forward. Although we couldn't really afford it, there was no way we were going to deny him the opportunity to do something that he loved to do. Period. Somehow, the bills would get paid. We were so far behind on a couple of them that missing one wouldn't have made much of a difference anyway.

Preparation for the Talent Inc. Showcase was basically the same as it was for the DeAbreu Modeling Extravaganza, just on a larger scale. Instead of one scene, Coy would have to learn three. Instead of six agents from Georgia, North Carolina, and New York, there would be over 30 from all over. Instead of 40 contestants, from Columbia, there would be over a hundred from 4 different states. He would also have to learn a special talent to perform. While Coy worked on getting ready to do what he had to do, Keisha and I worked on doing what we had to do to get him there. Which meant coming up with the money we needed for the entrance fee and travel expenses. We also had to buy new outfits for him to wear.

It took about four months of saving what we could and paying in installments, but we finally paid off the 1,900.00 with about two weeks to spare. In the meantime, Coy had been working hard on learning what he had to learn. He had decided to do a

Hip Hop dance for his special skill. The dance instructor from

DeAbreu came up with a cool dance that he was going to

perform to RUN DMC's *My Adidas.* Coy had taken some tap

dance lessons when he was younger but wasn't known as one

who could "cut a rug" as the old saying goes. Nevertheless, he

was adamant about doing it and worked hard on learning it. I

was really proud of him.

The time came for us to hit the road and head down to Orlando.

We had taken the six hour drive many times over the years.

Disney World was a regular vacation spot for us during Coy's

spring breaks over the years. The competition started on Friday

morning so we left on Thursday after Coy got out of school.

Although we didn't have to, we elected to stay at the hotel that

the showcase was being held at. We thought that it would be

easier to have to just go downstairs when it was time for the

competition as opposed to having to drive from another

location. The Hilton Orlando Resort Lake Buena Vista is a

beautiful hotel located right across the street from Downtown

Disney. Although we were on a tight budget, the discount we

got from being with the showcase made it possible for us to stay. We arrived that night and checked into our hotel at about 9. The workshops were scheduled to start at 9 the next morning so we got some dinner and hit the sack.

We walked into the ballroom the next morning at about 8:45. Coy had to get registered so we got there a few minutes early. The large room was half-filled with parents, kids, and agents, all milling around with excitement. Scott Cooper took the stage and introduced himself. He took about ten minutes giving us the history of his showcase and telling us what to expect over the next couple of days. After that, the kids participated in a series of workshops directed by some of the agents that were there. There were things like Walking the Runway, Acting for the Camera, and Booking the Audition, to name a few. This part of the weekend was just as big as the competition as far as we were concerned. There's nothing like learning something from someone who has actually done it.

There was a midday lunch break, more workshops, then

another two hour break for dinner before the modeling competition started. This took a few hours because there were so many contestants AND three different outfit categories. The special talent competition was also that night. Keisha had chosen a really cool old school Adidas sweat suit for Coy to wear during his routine. Of course I was nervous when he came out but again, he surprised me. He wasn't nervous or afraid at all. He did a really good job. When he was done, I told him that he had done well and asked if he was nervous at all."No. It was fun!" he said. "I know I'm not that good of a dancer but I wanted to see if I could do it. It was cool."Ok. Not sure if I could have put myself out there like that in front of 400 strangers when I was 10 years old but, ok.

The next morning, the acting competition began. For Coy, this is what it was all about. He accepted the fact that dancing wasn't his thing and just went out and did the best that he could. But this *was* his thing. He woke up that morning excited and anxious. He had a commercial, a monologue, and a film scene to do that day. Just like at the DeAbreu Extravaganza, all of the contestants had numbers pinned to their shirts. This time however, since there were so many of them, they would have 15 or so lined up right off stage according to the order in which they were calling numbers. As Coy got closer to the stage, my heart started beating faster and faster. I thought I was going to explode! My nervousness didn't stem from fear of him not doing well enough to get attention from some of the agents. I just didn't want him to mess up his lines or freeze up or do anything that would cause him to have a negative experience .Once he got on stage and started, I was put at ease yet again. He was great, and everyone knew it. There was a buzz in the room for a couple of minutes after he finished. As he made his way back to where we were sitting, he was stopped several times by different people congratulation him and telling him how good of a job he had done. I had seen some really talented kids go on before Coy but I had to admit, he stood out. There was something about him that was different. I couldn't put my finger on it, but it was there.

His second category was a film scene. We had been told that an acting coach who had conducted one of the workshops the day before would be reading lines with all of the contestants. He was also there as a representative of MC Talent Management in LA. When we found out who it was, Coy was beside himself. Patrick Malone. Yes, the same Patrick Malone from The Actor's Spot who had done the acting boot camp for the kids at DeAbreu the previous summer. The same one who had spoken such kind words about Coy after the boot camp was over. Patrick was there, not only to do a workshop and judge the competition, but also to look for talent for MC Talent to represent. I mentioned earlier that he spoke to his wife about Coy after he worked with him in Columbia, right? Ok...we'll get to that.

There's a huge difference between doing a monologue and doing a film scene with another actor. A monologue is performed alone. The actor is making a long speech. He or she may in fact be talking to someone, but they aren't necessarily interacting with them. Doing a scene with another actor is a different beast. Instead of just speaking words, you have to *listen* and *react* to what the other person is saying. I would imagine that Coy felt a certain level of comfort once he got on stage because he was familiar with Patrick and had enjoyed working with him before. In any case, he was amazing. To me anyway. Up to that point I had never seen him do an actual scene with another actor. I couldn't believe it. He blew me away. After he was done, there was another huge applause for him. Bigger than any other I'd heard all day. I remember thinking, "How did I not know he was this good at this??" After the film scene, he was done until after lunch so we decided to get away from it all for a little while. We took the boys to the pool and hung out. This was our plan from the beginning. Although we came so that Coy could participate in the Showcase, we wanted him to know that it wasn't necessarily about the competition. We wanted him to focus and do his best when it was time but this was another vacation for us. Nothing was predicated on his performance. We were going to have fun regardless!

We returned to the ballroom that evening for Coy's final

competition. The commercial scene. He was doing the same scene that he had done at DeAbreu so for the first time, I had some idea of how it was going to go. He blew everyone away again. After the last contestant, Scott Cooper spoke again and thanked everyone for making the showcase a success thus far. He explained what was going to take place the next day and then we were all dismissed. About thirty minutes after it was over, the ballroom was cleared out and they had a party for all of the kids. I thought it was a great way to end it. Most of them had been under a lot of pressure the past couple of days and it was good for them to be able to let off some steam.

At 8 o'clock on Sunday morning, they posted all of the callbacks from the agents. We were told to go down to the conference room area and that the information would be posted on the wall outside of the room where the competition was held. Each contestant had a three digit number that they wore while competing. Each agency would have their name on a sheet of paper which was taped to the wall. Under their name would be a list of three digit numbers, indicating which contestants they liked and wanted to meet with. I went down stairs with a pen and a sheet of paper, not really knowing what to expect. I thought that Coy had done well and I was proud of the way he worked leading up to the showcase. He had fun and did his best. That was all we could ask for. I really felt that anything beyond that was icing on the cake. So, on my way down to check out the callback list, I wasn't nervous or excited or anything. I got to the wall and looked at the first list and searched for number 310. It was there so I wrote that agency's name down and moved on to the second list. 310 again...and again...and again...and again. Out of the approximately 30 agencies that were represented, 14 of them had youth departments. Out of those 14, 11 had given Coy a callback. I headed back upstairs where the rest of the family was getting dressed (callbacks started at 9). I told everyone the good news, we celebrated for a minute, got dressed, and headed back downstairs for the actual callbacks.

The agents were set up in a huge conference room at individual tables. The process was that you simply went to the tables of the agents who had given your child a callback and spoke with

them. As we worked our way around the room meeting with

the 11 agents that had requested to speak with Coy, I quickly

realized that they were all using the same words and phrases in

describing what they saw in him: great look and personality,

very talented, natural, would be great for film, print, and

television. Of the 11, 5 were from New York, 5 were from Los

Angeles, and 1 was a modeling agency from Ocala, Florida. They

all said that they were interested in working with him and gave

us an open invitation to visit their agency.

After we met with all of the agents, we had about three hours

to kill until the awards banquet so we decided to take the boys

to the pool. On our way out, we ran into Josh Meeks one of the

organizers of the event who was also an agent at Wilhelmina

Evolution. He stopped us to tell us how proud he was of Coy and

asked us how many callbacks Coy had gotten. When we told

him 11, his reaction was...well, let's just say that he was REALLY

excited..."What?! Oh my God, are you serious?! 11?! In the ten

years we've been doing this we've never had anyone get more

that 3 or 4!! 11?! That's crazy!!"We didn't know until that moment how big a deal it was that so many of the agents liked Coy. It was our first time at the event so we thought that was normal.

The awards banquet started at 2 that afternoon. Everyone got all dressed up and we ate a nice meal before the ceremony started. They started with the modeling categories first, then moved on to the special talents before they got to the acting categories. In the middle of it all, my Keisha whispered in my ear..."I wasn't really thinking about it before but now I hope that Coy gets at least one trophy." She said. "I just don't want him to feel bad if he doesn't get anything.""Don't worry. I replied. "He will."

The first acting category was for the film scene. Coy's name was called first as the third place winner! Everyone cheered and we were all excited! As he went up to get his trophy, a sense of relief came over me. I hadn't let on, but what my wife had mentioned earlier had concerned me as well. It was never about winning or losing, but Coy had become more and more invested in the whole thing as the weekend went on. He wasn't concerned about winning a trophy but he felt that he had done his best and we thought that not winning anything might affect him. Now that he had gotten a trophy, Keisha and I were relieved. We could relax knowing that as far as Coy was concerned, the weekend had been a success.

Next up was the monologue category. Again, they started with the third place and called a kids name out. They then moved on to second place. When they got to the first place, I thought that I'd heard them say "Coy Stewart", but I was actually answering a question that Chayse had asked me. But when I looked up, Coy was already headed up to the stage. I thought, "Wow! This is better than we thought!" Next category: commercial. First place winner, Coy Stewart. It was ridiculous! They just kept...calling...his name. The more they called his name, the louder the cheers got. It was as if everyone in the room was excited for him.

Towards what I thought was the end of the awards, Chayse, had to go to the restroom. I got up and took him and as he and I were walking back into the conference room, everyone was standing up clapping and one of the other fathers who was sitting at our table was running up to me congratulating me. I thought to myself, "What is he congratulating me for? That was like 20 minutes ago." As I got further into the room, I looked up at the stage and Coy's picture was on the big screen. There was one last award that was given each year that Coy had also won. Best Overall Actor. Wow. Needless to say, I was excited, shocked, proud, all of the things you can imagine a parent would be at a time like that. What a great feeling to have your child accomplish something like that. More importantly than all of that, was how he reacted to it all. As we were leaving the conference room after all of the congratulatory gestures from everyone, this is what Coy said to us...

"When we get back to the room, can we say a prayer for all of my friends who didn't get anything? I feel bad for them."

We got back to the room and started preparing to head home. The night before, I had called one of my best friends from high school for a favor. We were in Orlando, Florida. Home of Mickey Mouse and all of his friends. How could we be there with a 10 year old and a 2 year old, and not take them to Disney World? The problem was we'd barely had enough money to get there in the first place and barely had enough to make it back home. I explained my situation to my friend and asked to borrow some money so that I could take my boys to Disney World and have enough gas to get back home. Being the friend that he is, he didn't hesitate to give me what I asked for. He transferred the money to our bank account immediately. So there we were, the parents of the Best Overall Child Actor at the 2008 Talent Inc. Showcase, borrowing money to take him to Disney world. We ended up not going because it rained for most of the day but it's still kind of ironic.

The trip home seemed to fly by. I had so much going on in my mind that I wasn't even thinking about the six hour drive. It was an exciting time and I kept trying to answer the question..."What next?" Like, where do we go from here? On one hand, hearing what the agents were saying about Coy made me excited about the possibilities that were out there. On the other, until something actually happened, it all meant nothing. So, where do we go from here? What's our next move? How do we just go back to Columbia and resume life as usual after all of this? How do we not? I had to come up with some sort of plan. I felt like we needed to be headed in a particular direction instead of just sitting around waiting.

4

NEW YORK CITY

A couple of days after we got home, Ericka called. She said that a few of the agents from NYC who had been in Orlando had called and invited some of her clients that they had seen in the showcase, to come to NYC to meet and discuss the future. Coy was one of the clients that had been invited. She was planning to make the trip with her group during spring break, which was a week away. Now, mind you, we were still trying to recover financially from the Orlando trip which we had just returned from a couple of days earlier. Keisha got paid every two weeks and had a payday coming up a in a couple of days. At the time, we had a car payment, insurance, and electric bills due. I'm sorry...past due. Not to mention a mortgage that was already in its second loan modification process. We decided to pay the electricity and insurance bills and save the rest for the trip. Gas, food, and lodging for the week in NYC was going to pretty much leave us tapped out when we returned but again, there was no way that we were not going to take him. So, a week later, we loaded up the truck and hit I95 North.

I made reservations at the Roosevelt Hotel in Manhattan on E 45th. All of Coys' appointments were in Manhattan so we figured it would be easier to get around. Hotels are a little more expensive in that area but with two kids in tow, we wanted to make it as easy as possible. While we were there that week, we met with three agencies, but there was always really only one choice for us. Heather Finn from Frontier Booking loved Coy from the moment she saw him at the DeAbreu Extravaganza. She is the agent who did the Q&A session before the Extravaganza started. She was also at the Talent, Inc. Showcase in Orlando.

When we met with her during the callback session in Orlando, she told us that she loved Coy, thought that he was very, very talented and would do very well in the business. She was one of the first agents we met with that day and the rest of the time we were in the callback session, every time we passed her table, she would look at us and mouth, "Pick me! I want him! I need him! Pick me!", which we thought was hilarious! But she clearly showed us that she really liked Coy and wanted to work with him.

She greeted us at her office in New York with the same level of enthusiasm. She introduced us to everyone in her office and told us that her colleague, John Shea was over their youth department and would be doing most of the work with Coy. We left her office and headed back to the hotel, which was only a few blocks away. We stopped at a McDonalds to get the boys something to eat and while we were in line, my phone rang. It was a NY area code so I answered. It was Heather and she asked me if I was interested in sending Coy on an audition while we were in town. I asked Coy and he said yes so I told her, "Sure." She said that she would call me back in 15 minutes. We changed our plans and ate our food there, waiting on her call. It took us about 25 minutes to eat and another 10 to make it back to the hotel. By the time we got up to the room, she still hadn't called so I thought that maybe it had fallen through. Of course, as soon as we got undressed, she called. She asked if we could be at an address in 20 minutes. I said "Sure." not knowing that we were 20 blocks away!

It was approximately ten minutes after 5 and we had to be there at 5:30. We rushed downstairs to hail a taxi , but as anyone who has tried to do that in NYC at that time of day can attest, we had a little difficulty. We started walking in the direction of our destination, hoping to catch a taxi along the way. There we were, a family of four that included a 10 year old, a 2 year old, and a stroller, rushing down 5th Avenue in Midtown Manhattan, trying to hail a taxi to take us to a destination that was now 15 blocks away, in 15 minutes! Needless to say, we had no luck whatsoever. We were headed in the direction we needed to go but every single taxi that passed us was already occupied. I looked at my watch and it was now 5:20 and we were still about 10 blocks away. Then, out of nowhere, a guy riding a bicycle that had a carriage attached

to it came riding down the street. Keisha and I looked at each

other at the same time. She gave me this look that said,

"Well, what do you think?"

I flagged the guy down and said to my family,

"Let's go!"

Coy looked at me like I was crazy.

"Dad, are you serious?!"

"Yeah! Let's go man. We've got to get there!"

So we all piled in and took off! Luckily, from that point on, we

were headed slightly downhill so the ride only took a few

minutes. We got to the building at 5:29 and rushed inside.

Once we got to the floor and room that we had been instructed

to go to, we walked into an empty waiting room. After a few

seconds, a very nice lady came out and introduced herself to us.

She then took Coy into her office for the audition. While they

were in there, I noticed a sign-in sheet on the table. I looked it

over and it was obvious that there had been auditions there for

pretty much the entire day. At the top of the sheet was the

name of a production company, and the title "The Sorcerer's

Apprentice". After a few minutes, they came out. She said that

Coy had done a wonderful job and that she would be in touch.

Great news as far as we were concerned. Whether he got the

part or not, we were happy that he had done such a good job.

Especially given the circumstances under which he arrived at

the audition. A very good friend of ours and the boys'

Godfather, Michael Curry, was the head coach of the NBA's

Detroit Pistons at the time. They just so happened to be in town

to play the Knicks so Madison Square Garden was our next stop.

We had a few minutes to kill so we stopped by the ESPN Zone in

Times Square to see the rest of the gang from DeAbreu who had

made the trip. They were about to have dinner so we visited

with them for a few minutes before heading to the game.

The next morning, we got up and got ready to head back to

South Carolina. We got a call from Heather who said that she

had just heard from the casting agent for The Sorcerer's

Apprentice. She didn't have any word on whether or not he had

gotten the part but was told that he was very talented and had done a great job. Great news to get before heading home!

Checking out of the Roosevelt, we encountered a problem similar to the one we had in Orlando: money. After paying for the hotel room and spending the week eating out for every meal, we had just enough to get back home. Which means that there was none left to pay the $200 valet parking bill we had accumulated during our five day stay. At forty bucks a day, I knew that we couldn't afford to pay it when we checked in. Unfortunately, there was nowhere else in the area to park overnight. So, I came up with an escape plan. In the hotel, there was a floor beneath the main floor that had various shops, a convenient store, barber, etc. There was also another exit on the other side of the hotel that led to 46th street. After we packed our things, we went to that bottom floor and I had Keisha and the boys wait for me by that door. I went to the valet desk and gave the guy standing there the ticket for our truck. He punched some keys on the computer.

"Ah, Mr. Stewart. Are you checking out now?"

"Not yet. I have to make a run but I will be checking out when I return."

"Very well sir. We'll have your vehicle brought around right away."

I think the rest of the story is pretty clear. It's not something I'm proud of but sometimes, you gotta do what you gotta do! They ended up charging our debit card a week later.

5

SUMMER PLANS

Once we returned to Columbia, things kind of went back to normal for a while. It was clear that Heather and Frontier Booking was the best fit for us. We called them upon our return and informed them that we would love to work with them. At that point, Ericka began discussing with us, and other parents, the possibility of taking our kids to New York or LA for the summer. While there are some opportunities in the North Carolina/South Carolina market for regional commercials and the occasional role as an extra in a movie, the truth is, a kid can go on more auditions in two weeks in LA or New York, than in 12 months in Columbia, SC or other smaller markets. Therefore, many people who don't live in New York or LA will take their kids to one of these cities for the summer, so that they can have more chances to audition for things. Ericka had taken her daughter Robyn to LA for the summer a couple of times. She said that it was a great experience for both Robyn and herself because it gave them some insight into the way the business works. Of course, you had to have representation in one of these cities in order to book auditions. There were agencies in both New York and LA who had been represented at the Orlando Showcase who had invited several kids from DeAbreu to come to their respective city for the summer.From there, the discussion came to be about which city we should go to. There was really no way to tell which would provide the best opportunity for our kids. Traditionally, January thru March is considered "Pilot Season" in LA. This is the time when studios and networks cast talent and shoot episodes for new sitcoms and dramas that could possibly be picked up for the fall season. It is common for hundreds of hopefuls to flock to LA during this time in hopes of landing a spot on a new show. The summer, however, is really kind of hit and miss. There are always roles for various movies, commercials, and print ads being cast, but you never really know what you're going to get. It was decided that for financial reasons, it would be easier to go to New York. The plan was to go from about the middle of June, until the end of July.

The next discussion was about the cost. After much research, we figured that with apartment rent, food, and money to get around the city, it would cost us approximately $5000.00 to do it. At that point, I had basketball camps, basketball clinics, and training sessions set up throughout the entire summer. We decided that Keisha would take a leave of absence and take the boys to New York, while I would stay back in Columbia and do my basketball stuff, which would allow me to provide them with the money they needed while they were there. It wasn't going to be enough to send them money AND pay all of our bills, but again, sometimes you gotta do what you gotta do.

Some people may think that we were making irresponsible decisions during this time but I never had any doubt that we were doing the right thing. I am a man of strong faith. Many years ago, I accepted Jesus Christ as my Lord and Savior and I know that he always has my back. The first thing I do every

morning is pray. I thank him for waking me and allowing me to

see another wonderful day he has created and I ask that he

guide me in the direction that he wants me to go. This gives me

confidence to go through my day knowing that I'm not walking

alone. I pray about the decisions I make and never second guess

or waiver. This is my take on bills: They will ALWAYS be there.

No matter where you live, what you do for a living, or how

much money you make, you will always have bills to pay. I have

never, nor will I ever, allow a bill to stop myself or my family

from doing something that is important to us. They're going to

cut our lights off? So what. It's not the first time for me. As a

kid, there were a few times that I got home from school and our

lights had been cut off. I'm still here. I survived it. I just feel like,

as long as you have a plan for where you're going and what

you're trying to accomplish, you'll be ok. You may have to, as

my mother use to say, "Rob Peter to pay Paul", but things will

work out.I have always approached life as a purposeful journey.

A trek to reach a certain destination or goal. Once that goal has

been reached, you set another one because otherwise, what are you living for? To simply get up in the morning, to go to work, to pay your bills so that you can have a place to eat and sleep, so that you can get up in the morning, go to work, so that you can pay your bills? I need more. I need to be working towards something. Otherwise, I don't feel alive. I don't know where it comes from. If I had to guess, I'd say that it comes from being an athlete my whole life. See, I fell in love with the game of basketball when I was about 11 or 12. I wasn't very good, but I loved to play. The fact that I was taller than most of my classmates, is what allowed me to play in junior high and be able to make the team once I got to high school. During my 9th grade year, I was terrible! Like I said, I made the team basically because I was very tall for my age but as far as skills, they were nonexistent. I was so bad that my teammates and other players would tease me right to my face!

At the end of the season that year, I seriously contemplated just quitting. The ridicule was that bad. But fortunately for me, God had delivered an angel into my life when I needed one most. See, my mother and step-father weren't very supportive of what I was doing. Don't get me wrong, they weren't against

it, they were just indifferent. Their main concern was putting

food on the table and keeping a roof over our head. But during

this time in my life, my maternal grandmother, Vertie Lou

Thomas, had come to live with us. She had recently suffered a

stroke that left her paralyzed on her left side. She came to live

with us so that she didn't have to live alone. We were very close

and had always been so. In fact, when I was very young, I

referred to her as "Mom", not "Grandma" as I did in later years.

She was very encouraging and supportive of everything I did.

When I told her that I was thinking of quitting the team because

I wasn't very good and I was tired of being teased, she told me

that if I really wanted to play, I shouldn't let anyone keep me

from doing that. Who were they to tell me that I wasn't good

enough? The coach must see something in me, otherwise, he

wouldn't have put me on the team. She told me that if I thought

I wasn't good enough, I would simply have to practice and get

better. So I did.

Every day after school, I would go to this court near my house. It was only a half court so no one really used it. I would come home from school, do my homework, and then go to the court for hours. There was a lamp post located right behind the basket so I would stay even after it got dark. There were many nights that my mother would have to send my brother out to get me. On the weekends, I would go to a gym and play pickup games with older guys. By the time we started practicing to go to basketball camp that summer, my skill level had surpassed that of all my teammates. I had a great summer camp and was promoted to varsity my sophomore year. It was during that time that I realized that if you work hard at something, you could actually better. That you could actually accomplish your goals if you were willing to pay the price.

Long story short, I ended up playing college basketball, leaving my school as the all time leading scorer and shot blocker, and playing professional basketball in Europe for ten years. Along the way, I continued to create goals, work hard to achieve them, and then create more goals. Goal #1-make varsity as a sophomore...done. Goal#2-earn a full athletic scholarship to attend college...done. Goal#3-play professional basketball...done. Goal#4-make it to the NBA...didn't get that one done, but worked my butt off trying. My life has been a series of goals. Setting them and being dedicated to reaching them. Without that, I'm lost. But what all of that taught me is that I can do anything I want to do if I believe, plan, and am willing to put in the work. This is what drives me and what I try to pass on to my boys. This is why I left my job at a mortgage company in 2004 and started coaching high school basketball. This is why I left that school and started my own basketball training company three years later. And this is why when my 10 year old son told me that he wanted to be an actor, my wife and I didn't hesitate to support him. This is also one of the reasons why I'm writing this book. It's another goal. Another challenge. Something else to work towards. Because otherwise, what's the point?

6

"IF YOU CAN MAKE IT HERE..."

So, New York for the summer. It worked out that Keisha and the boys were going to share a two bedroom sublet on the upper west side with two other mothers from DeAbreu, and their daughters. All told, there would be a total of eight people in the apartment, including another girl who's mother sent her, but couldn't come herself. On Friday, June 19th, we loaded up the truck...again, and headed up I95 North...again. We went to visit my family in Syracuse, NY that weekend for Father's Day first then headed to the city on Monday. When we got there, everyone else was already in the apartment. I got them settled and headed back down I95 south...again!

It was a difficult six weeks for me to say the least. We have always been a very close knit family and I was miserable without them. I kept myself busy with my basketball camps, skills clinics, individual training sessions, etc, but it was always hard to come home afterwards. When the boys are home, there is always so much energy in the house. But they were gone and the house was soulless. Dead. Keisha wasn't walking around laughing on the phone or in the kitchen cooking. The boys weren't chasing each other around the house, screaming at the top of their lungs. There was nothing. I would never admit this to them, but whenever I wasn't watching television, I would keep it on The Disney Channel, just to make if feel like they were there. We would talk on the phone several times a day, especially before, and after Coy's auditions. Before we left, we had a conversation with Coy similar to the one we had before the Orlando Showcase. The goal is to go into these auditions and do the best you can. That's it. If you book it, great, if not, it wasn't for you and we move on to the next one. We told him to look at each audition as an opportunity to prepare for the next audition. With each one, you get better and better so that when you get to the one that *is* for you, you'll be ready. Coy has always seemed to have a great outlook on this. He was never fazed when he didn't book a job. It never affected him negatively because he never had any doubt that he was going to be doing what he's doing. Whenever he went in for an audition that he didn't get, he would always just say "That's ok. That one wasn't mine. Mine is coming."

During their six week stay, Coy went on about two or three auditions a week. Mostly for print ads but there were some commercial auditions sprinkled in there as well. He got a lot of callbacks but never booked anything. There were a couple of times when I talked to him on the phone that he broke down a little bit but never because of not booking jobs. He was missing me and missing home. He was out of his element, away from his father, away from home, staying in an apartment full of girls. Sometimes, he would get frustrated. But we would talk and I would tell him that it was only temporary. That he had a goal that he was trying to reach and sometimes, it wouldn't be easy. That sometimes in order to do things that other people can't, you have to be willing to do things that other people won't. In the end, he stuck it out, and it paid off.

About four days before I was scheduled to head back up I-95 to pick them up, Coy got an audition for a play. "**A Raisin in the Sun**" was scheduled to run for six weeks at the Weston Playhouse Theater in Weston, Vt. They were casting the play in NY and Coy was scheduled to audition for the part of Travis Younger. This was on a Friday and they emailed the sides[10] so that he could prepare for the audition, which was on Monday. Coy was really excited and said that he really wanted to do this play. He and I were on the phone several times over the weekend, working on his lines. On Monday, I talked with him and Keisha before, and after the audition. When it was over, they were both really excited. Coy said that he felt really good about his performance. Keisha told me that after Coy was done, they called her in and introduced themselves to her. They asked her a few questions about our availability to bring Coy to Vermont, school, etc. We got off the phone and went on our way. A couple of hours later, I got a call from John Shea at Frontier Booking, who had sent Coy on the audition in the first

---

[10] *Sides-Parts of a script that actors use to audition. Usually sent to the actor or his agent by the casting director. They can also refer to the lines that an actor will be doing on set on any given day. If this is the case, the sides will be in the actor's dressing room when they arrive to set.*

place. He said that they loved Coy and would like to offer him the role! I immediately called Keisha and told them the good news. We were all sooo excited! He was about to do a play! An actual professional play! Wow.

At that point, it was time to bring them home. I moved my timetable up a couple of days and left on Wednesday to pick them up. We were scheduled to be in Weston on August 5th, which was about a week and a half away. Over the next few days, I shared a series of emails and faxes with John concerning the contracts associated with Coy doing the play. In addition to Coy's weekly pay, they would provide us with a two bedroom cottage during the duration of the play. While all of that was being taken care of, we were busy getting everything in order so that we could be gone for five weeks.

The first priority was working something out with Coy's school. He was about to start the 6th grade in a magnet program at a public school. I met with the administrator over the program and explained our unique situation. Coy would miss the first two months of school because of the play. He was scheduled

to rehearse for three weeks, perform it at the Weston

Playhouse Theater for two weeks, have a two week hiatus, and

then go on tour for two weeks. Unfortunately, the school wasn't

very supportive. I was told that if he wasn't at school within the

first ten days, he would be removed from the magnet program

and his spot would be given to someone else. Fortunately, we

had a fallback. Coy had also been accepted into a private school.

Heathwood Hall Episcipol School was a great school and the

only reason we had chosen the magnet school program in the

first place is because it seemed like he would be basically

getting the same education for free.

I called the private school and set up a meeting with the head of

admissions. After seeing her reaction to our situation, it was

clear that this was going to work out. She was so excited! She

told us that Monique Coleman of Disney's *High School Musical*

was a former student and that they were very proud of her.

They encouraged all of their students to strive to achieve their

goals and always helped in any way they could. The process was simple: I would meet with all of Coy's teachers and they would provide me with all of the books and materials he needed. They would email me Coy's assignments on a weekly basis and I would email or mail them in at the end of each week. Perfect! Got that taken care of.

The next thing was convincing my wife that she had to come with us. The first thing Coy said when I told them that he had gotten the part, was that he needed all of us to go. He said that he couldn't do this without his entire family and if we all couldn't come, he didn't want to go. It wasn't that Keisha didn't want to go. Of course she did. But as I said earlier, at that time, she was the primary breadwinner in the household and felt a certain financial responsibility to the family. Not to mention the fact that she was just ending a six week leave of absence. We talked about it, prayed about it, and I just told her that she didn't really have a choice. Coy said that he needed all of us to be there. We have to go. Period. So...we loaded up the truck and we moved to Beverly...Hills that is...swimming pools, movie stars! (sorry, I couldn't resist). Anyway, we headed up north...again! This time we were going to be gone for about 5 weeks. We went to Syracuse, NY again for the weekend before heading to Vermont.

7

RAISIN

Weston, Vermont is a beautiful, small town located in the
southwestern part of Vermont set in the midst of winding
country roads lined with beautiful trees and homes that seemed
to have been lifted off of a postcard. It is home to the famous
Vermont Country Store and of course the Weston Playhouse
Theater. We arrived the day before they started rehearsals. The
people in Weston and those who work for the theater company
are some of the nicest people in the world. We could tell as
soon as we arrived that this was going to be a great experience
for the whole family. We were greeted by the company
manager at the time, MB Makara. She is one of the sweetest,
most caring people in the world and she made us feel at ease
right away. She took us where would we be staying which was a
nice two bedroom cottage right on the edge of town. The

owners had recently had it renovated and had graciously offered it to the company for us to stay in during the run of the play. It was perfect for us.

We got settled and the next day took Coy to the rehearsal hall to meet the rest of the cast and have their first table read[11]. The rehearsal hall was unique because it was actually a three story house with several bedrooms on the upstairs levels. Most of the cast stayed here. An addition had been added on to the back of the house and was used as a rehearsal area when there was another production going on in the theater, as was the case when we got there. It was at this point that I got a little nervous. See, from the time we found out that Coy had booked this job, it was all about the excitement of it and doing what we had to do to get here. But now that we were here, it hit me...this is a real job! Not a school play or a church program. A real, live, professional play. At a real theater. With real, professional actors. He was already the only child in the entire cast but he

---

[11] Table Read-When the script of a play, film, or tv episode is read in its' entirety by the cast for purposes of familiarity and timing.

was also the only one who had no experience. None. Was he ready for this? Was he going to be nervous? He had never done a table read before and he was about to do his first one with professional adult actors who had been doing it for years. So yeah, I was a little nervous.

Fortunately, everyone from the cast and director, to the stage manager, seemed to be really nice when we met them. When they went in to do the table read, I decided to stay out of the room. I had never seen the play and I really wanted to experience it, and Coy, for the first time with as fresh a set of eyes as possible. So I sat in the living room while they did the table read. After about two hours, they came out for a break. Two of the cast members, Wendell Franklin and Raphael Peacock, asked me if I would like to walk across the street and get a cup of coffee with them. As we talked over coffee, one of them asked how long Coy had been acting. When I told them that he had really just started and this was actually his first job, they couldn't believe it.

"Man, ya'll better get ready for this ride." Said Wendell.

"What do you mean?" I asked.

"That kid is going to be a star." He said.

"Really? You think so? " I asked.

"No. I KNOW so. Trust me. I've been doing this for a while." He said.

Rahpael shook his head, agreeing with Wendell. "Yeah, he's got IT. And don't ask me what IT is 'cause I don't know. But I do know that he's got it."

"So how's he doing in there? I was a little nervous because this is his first table read." I asked.

"Man, it's like he's been doing it his whole life." Wendell responded.

" Yep." added Raphael.

" I've worked with adult actors that he would just blow out of the water." Wendell said.

"Wow." I responded. " Ok. Well that's good to know. I'm just glad he's not in over his head."

"Man, let that be the least of your worries." Wendell replied. " Ya'll just better get ready for this ride he's about to take you on."

After this conversation, I felt a little more at ease. I mean, these

guys were actors so I figured they knew a little about what they were saying. But at that time, I didn't really process what they had said about him being a star and getting ready for this "ride he's about to take you on". I was just happy that for the time being, he was doing ok. That he wasn't in over his head.

Before we left to head to Vermont, Keisha and I had a conversation about the play and how it would impact Coy. After seeing his schedule, I told her that we were going to find out if this is really what he wanted to do. Up until that point, he hadn't really done anything. A couple of talent showcases and standing around as an extra on a movie set. Nothing like what he was about to embark on. Once in Weston, he would rehearse for 8 hours a day for three weeks Monday thru Friday and then do school work after. Once the play actually started its run, he had six shows a week. They would perform Tuesday thru Saturday nights plus a matinee on Saturday afternoon. This was a pretty grueling schedule but it's somewhat typical of what the theater industry is like. Table reads and rehearsals are a part of the job. We figured that if he came out of this still wanting to be an actor, we were in this for the long haul.

Once they started, he would come home exhausted at the end

of the day, but he never complained and he was always excited

to get back the next day. He was having a ball. The only issue we

had was school. There was an adjustment period that was

somewhat difficult for him. It was tough for him to be working

on the play for eight hours during the day, collaborating with

other actors and doing what he loved to do, and then have to

switch gears and focus on school. It took some getting used to

but he eventually found a way to do it. I would explain to him

that he wasn't in this alone. I understood how it could be

frustrating for him but he didn't have a choice. It all goes back

to being willing to do what you have to do so that you can do

what you want to do.

This was a really good time for our family. I would tell Keisha

that it was very similar to us being in Europe when I was playing

basketball. We were away from our home and didn't know

anyone except for the people associated with the theater

company. This kind of forced us to rely on each other and as a result, brought our family closer than we already were. We would spend all of our time away from the theater together. We would take rides to Rutland, which was a bigger city about 30 miles away. There was a mall, a movie theater, wider selection of restaurants, things like that. We would go to another small town about 15 minutes away to do laundry. We would also spend time with the other cast members and some of the people who worked for the company, like MB, whom I mentioned earlier. They all turned out to be really good people. Some of whom we are still friends with to this day.

After three weeks of rehearsals, premiere night had finally arrived. I was just as nervous as I was when he performed at the DeAbreu Extravaganza and at the Orlando Showcase! You'd think that I would have been use to it at that point. But now I felt even more nervous than I had been at those two previous shows. This was theater. People take this stuff seriously! There would be a live audience and reviews and all the normal trimmings of a stage production. Up to this point, he had been doing great with rehearsal and everything but things were about to get real now. Anyway, that's how I was feeling. Coy on the other hand...well, let's just say that either he didn't realize the magnitude of what he was about to do, didn't care, or simply wasn't fazed by it. I was starting to think that maybe this is what this kid is supposed to be doing. The closer we got to curtain call, the more excited he got. He admitted later that he had just a small bout of nervousness right before the curtain went up, but it only lasted a few seconds.

Because Coy was a minor, the theater was required to have a child wrangler [12] on set. This person's job was to take care of Coy during the performance. They would stay with him at all times, make sure that he had on the proper wardrobe for his next scene, and walk him to and from the stage when it was time. Keisha and I were always down in the green room as well. It was relaxing and we could hear the play because it was piped in via speakers. On this night though, we wanted to experience it in the audience. This was our son's first time on stage. We had no

---

[12] *Child Wrangler-An adult who is responsible for minors who are a part of a stage production, movie, or tv production.*

idea what it would lead to and wanted to be sure that we got the full experience.

The night was a huge success. The play (which I had never seen) was great and the entire cast was wonderful. I had never been to a play before. Never really wanted to. Again, another way in which this was a great experience for all of us. I'm a big movie buff so I love going to the movie theater or even watching a good movie at home. But the theatre is a much more intimate experience. I absolutely loved it! So not only did I get to see my son excel in his first performance but also I got to see a great play, something that may have never happened if Coy hadn't gotten into this business. The play opened to great reviews and Coy did a wonderful job. This was actually a great play for him to start on because his role was not that big so he didn't have a lot of lines but he was on stage quite a bit. It was also great for him to be around professional actors. He got to see how they rehearsed and how they prepared before each show. It was a really great learning experience for him. Something he can't really get in an acting class.

During the opening scene, something funny happened that could be a precursor to coming events. Chayse, who was about to turn 3 at the time, was sitting in Keisha's lap when the curtain rose on the opening act. This was Coy's first scene and when he started saying his lines, Chayse started saying them along with him! And not just saying them, but yelling them as if he wanted to make sure Coy could hear him! Horrified, Keisha immediately put her hand over his mouth but he pulled it away and continued saying the lines. She had to get up and take him out of the theater! Obviously we were embarrassed. But later, we realized that he actually knew all of the lines, word for word. Not only did he know them, but he knew *when* and *how* to say them. This was interesting to us because apparently, he had been listening when Coy worked on his lines. But we had no idea.

As the play went on, we started to get more and more feedback about Coy from people associated with the theater and those who were simply coming to see it. It all sounded the same: he's so talented; he's so natural; he so well spoken; he's going to be a star, etc. For me, the compliments were nice. I mean who wouldn't want to hear those kinds of things about their child? But I was always thinking in terms of him doing this long term. Therefore, as nice as the compliments that came from audience members were, I was more focused on the ones that came from people who were involved in theater in some capacity. See, they would have a better understanding of how good he really was as it relates to his potential for success in the industry.

As we got closer to the end of the run of the play in Weston, I started to think about the long term future. It was beginning to look like Coy had a chance to actually make a career of this and I just felt like the best way for us to help him do that was to put him in a position to have as many opportunities as possible. Translation: we needed to move. Columbia, SC, as nice a city as it is, is not known as a hotbed for acting. If Coy wanted to be an actor, we needed to go where that particular industry was located...Hollywood!

It may seem crazy to some but it was perfectly logical to me. I just believe in going after what you want. When I got out of college, I wanted to play professional basketball. I didn't have an opportunity to do that here in the U.S., so I went where I did have an opportunity...Europe. Again, it's all about my philosophy on life. You've got to have something that drives you forward. A goal. A purpose. If Coy's goal was to be an actor, our goal would become doing what we needed to do to help him achieve that.

But first, we had to check out the landscape. We needed to see if LA was a place that we would actually like to live. We had a two week break coming up after the Weston run of the play, before we went on the two week tour. I talked to Keisha and told her what I had been thinking about. I suggested that we take a trip out west during this break and check out the landscape. Look at different areas, check out schools, etc. See if we could actually live there. Also, I thought we could set up meetings with some of the agents that we met at the Talent Inc Showcase back in the spring. We could talk with them and tell them of our plans to move. See what they thought of Coy's chances of getting work out there. She agreed so I set the wheels in motion.

I called a couple of the agencies myself, reminded them of who I was, and set up meetings. I also called Ericka DeAbreu and told her of our plans. She called a couple agencies and set up appointments as well. I began researching flight, hotel, and rental car information as well. We would spend a total of six days there and meet with five agencies and one talent management firm during that time. Coy's last performance was on Friday morning and we had planned to head back to SC immediately after. I figured we would leave for LA on that Monday, return on Saturday, and have a week at home before Coy and I returned to Vermont for the tour.

8

CITY OF ANGELS

Keisha got paid on the Friday that we were to head back to SC.
That morning before we headed to Coy's last performance, I
told her that I was going to go ahead and purchase our airline
tickets for Monday, and pay for our hotel in LA. Now, we had
already had a conversation about all of this a couple of weeks
earlier. But once it was time to actually spend the money it was
going to take to do it, she got cold feet.

"Is this what we really need to be doing right now?" she asked.
"There are other things we could be doing with this paycheck."
"Keisha, we already discussed this. This is *exactly* what we need
to be doing. We have to start looking forward. We'll pay the
electricity and water bills but everything else can wait. We

need to go do this *now*."

"I'm just saying. What are we really going to accomplish?"

"We're going out here to meet with these agents to see if they

think Coy could have some success out there. Plus, we need to

check the city out and see if we could actually live out there."

"I understand that but why now?" she asked. "Shouldn't we
wait?"

"Wait for what??" I asked. "What is there to wait for? We need

to go now and see what's what. This trip is going to determine

how we move forward from here."

"Alright, alright." She said. "As long as you've thought about it

and taken everything into consideration."

"I have." I replied. "We're good. Trust me."

This is not a negative reflection of my lovely wife. In fact, this is

the reason we work so well together. There's a great balance in

our relationship because I push and encourage her to try things

that she probably wouldn't otherwise and she keeps me

grounded in certain situations by making me take some things

into consideration that I might not otherwise. She was not

against what I was suggesting. Her concern was simply that we were making the right decision financially for the family.

So we headed back to SC on Friday after Coy's matinee performance. Before we got on the road, I called and paid our water bill at our house Columbia. The water had been turned off earlier in the week. They said that they would send someone out that day to turn it back on. We weren't going to be home until Saturday morning so it was cool. The problem was that they wouldn't turn the service back on if there was no one was home. This policy was in place to avoid the possibility of water damage if someone had left a faucet or something on and their water service was turned back on while they were not there. So it turns out that even though we had paid the bill, they couldn't turn it back on because we weren't there when they came out.

We arrived home on Saturday morning to no running water in our house. Imagine driving all night and then getting home and not being able to take a shower! Ewww! It was a little rough to say the least. I called the water department when they opened and they said that someone would be back out that day...at some point...before 5pm. So we just hung out around the house all day which really wasn't that bad. We basically slept most of the day off and on because we were still tired form the drive. Some people may have been frustrated and upset all day, but I tend to look at the big picture in all situations. Yes, we didn't have water at the house which meant that we couldn't take showers, or use the bathroom. But we had just returned from Weston, Vt where our oldest son had just finished performing in his first professional play. In two days, we would head to LA for a week to meet with several agents about the possibility of moving out there so that said son could pursue an acting career. While that particular moment that we were in may have seemed bleak, the future was bright!

On Monday, we left for LA. We were all pretty excited. When I did research on hotels, I obviously looked for the best deal financially. It appeared that the further the hotels were from the city, the better the prices. I ended up booking us at the Residence Inn in Anaheim, CA. According to the information on the website I was on, it was approximately 22 miles from downtown LA. Now, taking into consideration that we had to drive into town every day, I thought that for the price of our room, 22 miles wasn't that bad. It's about 20 minutes on the highway. Now, for those of you who live in or have spent time in LA, you know that I had NO IDEA what I was talking about. The most direct route from Anaheim to LA is on interstate 405. 22 miles. 20 minutes, right? Wrong! Let me see if I can describe traffic on the 405...sorry, I can't. There is no explanation for a highway that has traffic congestion ALL THE TIME! No, really. When I say all the time, I literally mean ALL THE TIME. There were times when we were traveling on the 405 at eleven o'clock at night...and there was traffic congestion! So what should have been a 20-25 min ride turned out to be a 45-60 minute ride each way. But hey, that's why we were there, to learn these things right? (See how I look at things...big picture.)We got settled at the hotel on Monday night and I plotted out our trip for the next day.

We had one meeting on Tuesday with an agency in Beverly Hills.

We figured that for the rest of the day we would do some sightseeing and look at some areas in which we could possibly live. The agency was pretty easy to find and I made sure we left early enough to have plenty of time to get there. Ericka DeAbreu had given me the information about the meeting and we found out later that it was actually set up by Patrick Malone. We got there about ten minutes early and were greeted by one of the assistants. She gave Coy a script to work on and prepare for a cold read[13]. This is typical when meeting with an agency for possible representation.

We were directed to an empty office and told that he would have a few minutes to prepare and then they would come and get him. In the script, his character was supposed to run and jump onto a school bus, as if he had barely made it before the bus left. I remembered Coy telling me about something he had learned in the acting boot camp he did at DeAbreu with Patrick. He told me that Patrick said that if you are in an audition and

---

[13] *Cold Read-Auditioning with a script that you've never seen before without any practice or rehearsal.*

the character is suppose to be performing a particular action, you should perform that action(to the best of your ability) while saying your lines. I reminded Coy of this. So when he went in the office to audition, he ran and jumped, as if he were landing on a bus like the character he was reading. They loved it.

They called me in when he was done and introduced themselves. There were three agents in the office, two female, one male. I'm going to list the comments that were made to me about Coy. As I continue to describe the meetings with the different agencies during the week, you'll start to see a pattern: *"We love him; he's very talented; very natural; he's got a great look; he would be great for film and tv; we don't have anyone like him on our client roster so he would be the only African-American boy his age in the agency; he would start working right away; we would love to work with him."*

When I mentioned that we were considering moving to LA, they got excited and said that if we decided to do that, there was no doubt that he would start working right away.

Once we were done, we left and just kind of drove around the area for a while. Just kind of getting a feel for the place. We ended up on Hollywood Blvd and got a chance to see the walk of stars which was kind of cool. We also checked out a couple of neighborhoods that we had researched on the internet and hit a famous restaurant (Roscoe's Chicken and Waffles) that I had heard a lot about.

The next day we had two meetings. One with a talent manager in North Hollywood, and one with an agency in Calabasas, just north of LA. Earlier in this book, I mentioned that Patrick Malone had told his wife about Coy when he returned home from doing the acting boot camp in Columbia. Here's the reason I mentioned it: His wife, Jamie Malone, is the owner of MC Talent Management. We met her and Patrick at a cafe in North Hollywood that morning. She was very nice and spoke very highly of Coy. She told us that Patrick had raved about Coy when he returned from doing the acting boot camp and told her that she had to sign him. She had seen him up close and personal at the DeAbreu Extravaganza and thought he was:

"he's very talented; very natural; he's got a great look; he would be great for film and tv; we don't have anyone like him on our client roster so he would be the only African-American boy his age in the agency; he would start working right away; we would love to work with him."

She was also the manager of Ericka's oldest daughter and had worked with them during the summers that they spent in LA. She mentioned that we could start off the same way and that it was also possible to put Coy on tape for certain auditions, with the knowledge that we would have to bring him out to LA for any callbacks. We mentioned that we were tossing around the idea of moving out to LA and she thought that it was a great idea. She said that she had no doubt that he would start working right away.

An hour later, we were on our way to meet with another agency located in Calabasas. We had also met with one of their agents in Orlando. They were also very nice and took Coy back in the office alone initially while I sat in the waiting area. After a few minutes, they came and got me...

"he's very talented, very natural, he's got a great look, (one of them even said that he was so good looking, that he was almost pretty!) he would be great for film and tv, we don't have anyone like him on our client roster so he would be the only African-American boy his age in the agency, he would start working right away, we would love to work with him." Clearly, they liked him.

We obviously started to see a pattern in what we were being told about him. This pattern lead us to one obvious conclusion: he had a legitimate shot at success in this business. We had two more meetings over the next couple of days that basically went the same way. The one thing I noticed about all of these agencies is that none of them asked us what other agencies we were meeting with. There were no negative comments about one being better than the other or horror stories about rival agencies. They all just talked about what they had to offer and how they would love working with us. I liked that.

When we weren't meeting with agents, we were exploring the city. I had been to LA back in college but it was a basketball related trip and I didn't really have a chance to see it. We tried to explore the area as much as possible to get a feel for whether or not we could see ourselves living there. None of what we were doing would matter if this wasn't a place that we wanted to be. We naturally went to a couple of the tourist stops-Hollywood Blvd., Grauman's Chinese Theatre, etc.-but we also checked out some of the neighborhoods like Calabasas, Woodland Hills, Sherman Oaks, and Studio City to name a few.

At the end of the week, we headed back to South Carolina. It had been a very successful trip in my mind because I felt that we left with a better understanding of what we were dealing with. It's one thing to be in SC, thinking about what the business was really like in LA and wondering if Coy had what it takes to make it. Hearing all of the compliments from people in Vermont associated with the play made me think...maybe. But spending time in LA confirmed it for me. Being out there in that world that seemed to be calling. Hearing from people who actually make a living doing this. It just made me it all real for me. Like

this could *actually happen*.

9

THE RAISIN TOUR

After a week in SC, Coy and I headed back to Vermont. It was time to embark on the two week tour of *A Raisin in the Sun*. The tour was scheduled to take us through several small towns in Vermont and Massachusetts, which I thought would be a wonderful experience for Coy. Keisha and Chayse didn't travel with us on the tour. It was going to be too difficult for a 2 year old to endure so they stayed home. We met back up with everyone in Weston and set off on our excursion! There were a total of 11 of us divided into two vans-a 15 passenger and a minivan. I was the designated driver of the 15 passenger van. I volunteered because, well, I wasn't doing anything else. Besides, it was a lot of fun.

The schedule was pretty tough but we were with a great group of people so there weren't any major issues. It was kind of like being on a road trip when I played basketball. We would arrive in a town, check into our hotel, grab some food, head to the theater, the cast would perform, we'd grab some dinner to take back to the room, eat, sleep, wake up early in the morning, check out, and hit the road again, headed to the next destination. Coy also had to do school work every day in between all of this. The longest distance we drove at one time was probably three hours so it wasn't bad. Unfortunately, I can't say the same about some of the hotels that we stayed in along the way. They were *interesting* to say the least. There was one Motor Lodge in particular in a small town in Vermont that was really...vintage. You actually had to change the channel on the television manually. Coy thought that was outrageous! It was really fun seeing his reaction to the places we were going. But it was a great experience for him. A few of the venues were actually places where drama clubs from local high schools would come see the play. Afterwards, the cast would do a Q&A session with the students. I was always impressed and proud of the way Coy handled himself during these sessions. There he was, the only child in the production, sitting onstage with the rest of the actor's answering questions like this was something he did all the time. I have to say...it was pretty impressive.

On the last stop of the tour, we were in a larger city so we were able to stay in a Marriott hotel. We checked in and when we got to our room, Coy walked in like he had arrived at his dream house.

"Ahh, now this is what I'm talking about!"

He walked over to one of the walls, leaned on it, and began talking...to the wall.

"Man, it's so good to see you Marriott. Can you believe they had me staying at the Ramada Inn?! Crazy right?? I know!!"

They had a performance at 9:30 the next morning and then that was it. The tour was over. That morning, I dropped everyone off at the theater and then headed back to our hotel for breakfast. I ended up eating with one of the managers of the theater who had come to see the last performance. We were talking and he asked about our plans after the play. I mentioned to him that

we were considering moving to LA so that Coy could continue to

pursue his dream. He said that he hoped that Coy would still

come back to The Weston Playhouse to do plays after he

becomes a big star. I kind of laughed and said that "if" Coy ever

becomes a big star, he will always want to come back to Weston

to work because he had a great time. He then looked me

straight in the eye with a serious look on his face...

"No, it's not "if" he becomes a star, but "when" he becomes a

star. It's only a matter of time and you and Keisha need to

realize that because your whole life is going to change".

He had such a serious look on his face that I knew that he truly

 believed what he was saying to me.

After the tour was over, we returned to South Carolina. At this

point, I was convinced that the right move was for us to relocate

the family to LA. I had been praying about it a lot and I just felt

that staying in Columbia at that time was pointless. Some

people may have looked at it and thought that I was crazy. Just

pick up and move to LA?? But to me, it was perfectly logical. As I said earlier, I have always believed in going after what you

want. That's what life is all about. Coy wanted to be an actor.

Let's go.

10

THE

CONVERSATION

See, for me, when it comes to situations like this, I always think about worst case scenario. What's the worst thing that can happen in a situation with which you are faced? If you can survive that, then you'll be ok. In this situation, the worst case scenario was...we move to LA, Coy starts auditioning for different things, a year or two later he hasn't made any progress whatsoever. Now, we just live in LA. We could always come back to Columbia. That was the worst case scenario. Clearly we could survive that so there was no reason in my mind not to do it. On our trip home, I talked to Coy about his experience in

Vermont. I wanted to know if he'd truly enjoyed it and if this was something he still wanted to do. He was sooo excited and said that the play was fun and he wanted to do a tv show now. I asked him how he felt about moving to LA. His response?

"Can we?!"

Now all I had to do was convince Keisha. A couple of days after Coy and I got home from Vermont, I decided to attack! We were putting sheets on our bed and I thought that this was as good a time as any.

"Keisha, let me ask you a question."

"Ok."

" The play is over and we're back, what do we do now?"

"What do you mean?"

"I mean, Coy is an actor, right?"

"Right."

"I, mean, he's gone from *trying* to be an actor, to being an actor, right?"

"Right."

"And where do most actors live?"

"In LA." she replied.

" Right."

"So are you saying that we should consider moving to LA?" she

asks.

"Not *consider* moving to LA. I don't think there's anything to

consider. If this is what he wants to do, that's where we need

to be. Right?"

"Right."

"Look, the company you work for has got stores and call centers

in LA." You've been with them for 10 years. It shouldn't be a

problem for you to transfer your job somewhere out there. I'll

start putting out feelers through the YMCA and look for a

position with them. We can look for an apartment initially and

just take it from there."

The look on her face told me that I had her. She didn't put up

any kind of resistance or show any major concern. All she

needed at this point was to know that I had really thought

about all of this and planned it out.

"What do we do about this house?" she asked.

"I've been praying about this whole situation." I told her.

"We're going to get it ready to put on the market. We'll either
sell it, or rent it out. Whatever God's will is what will be."

"So how soon are you talking about?" she asked.

"Like, immediately." I said. "Let's start the process right now."

"What if we wait until the summer?" she asked."Let Coy finish
out the school year here and give ourselves time to get
everything together."

"No, the time is now." I told her. "It's October. If we start the
process now, we can be ready to move at the beginning of the
year. It's perfect because pilot season starts in LA in January."

"Ok. Let's do it." She said. "Why not? There's nothing going on
here."

We talked to Coy and told him what we were considering. He
was really excited. We told him that we would go out and let
him do his thing and see what happens. And that was that. The
Stewart's were moving to LA.

Once the decision was made, the next step was to come up with
a plan of attack. I made a checklist of things that needed to be

done. Start looking for an apartment, start looking into junior high schools, start making contact with LA area YMCA's to look for employment, look for a real estate agent to assist in selling our home, contact Coy's manager and agency in LA to let them know that we would be permanently relocated there at the beginning of the year, do an assessment of the house to determine what needed to be done to get it market ready, (Keisha) start the process of transferring her job to LA. Whew! So as you could see, we had a lot of work to do in a relatively short period of time. But, it was cool because it gave us goals to work towards.

11

COMMERCIAL INTURRUPTION

In the midst of all of this, Coy was sent on an audition by Ericka DeAbreu. It was for a regional commercial and the audition was on a Friday in Charlotte, North Carolina. I like thinking about this story because it's another example of how Keisha and I refused to let our financial limitations stop us from helping our son realize his dreams. I had to drive the approximately 70 miles to Charlotte to take Coy to the audition. Keisha couldn't go because she had to work. So it was just me and the boys. I had a little over a quarter of a tank of gas in the car and a twenty dollar bill in my pocket. Keisha wasn't getting paid until the next day. I'll never forget this day because I had spoken to Palmetto Utilities earlier that day. Palmetto Utilities was who we paid our sewer fees to every month. We were really behind at that point and they were scheduled to cut our service at some point that day. From what they told me, this process involved digging up some portion of our yard so during the whole trip to Charlotte and back, I was wondering if we would get home to a big hole in our front yard. How was I going to explain that to the boys? Anyway, there was nothing I could do about it at that point. They wouldn't take a check which meant that we wouldn't be able to pay it until the next morning, so that was that. I prayed about it (really just to have a certain level of peace) and headed to Charlotte.

When we left the audition, I had planned to put the twenty dollars in the gas tank to get home, but the boys said that they were hungry. So, we stopped at Chick-Fil-A and I got them some food. After that, I had 9 dollars left. I put that in the tank and it was just enough to get us home. The lady at Palmetto Utilities said that if they didn't get to our house before 5 that day, they would be out the next day to disconnect our service. We got back to our neighborhood at about ten after six. I turned the corner and headed down the street towards our house, wondering what I was going to find. As our front yard came into view, I looked to see if anything had changed. The closer I got, I realized that it hadn't. Apparently, they didn't get to us that day! Another bullet dodged! Keisha's salary was direct deposited into our account that night and the first call I made the next morning was to Palmetto Utilities. By the way, we found out on that Monday that Coy had booked the commercial!

We had to take him back to North Carolina on the following Wednesday night for a Thursday morning shoot. It was a regional commercial for CarQuest. The whole family made the trip so it was a lot of fun. They got us a hotel room for Wednesday night so we checked in as soon as we got there. We didn't leave Columbia until Keisha got home from work so it was kind of late by the time we got there. We got some dinner and then went to bed because Coy had a 7am call time [14]the next day.

---

[14] *Call Time-The time that actors or crew members are required to report to set. This time varies from day to day.*

The next morning, Keisha and Chayse took Coy and me to the set which was actually at someone's house in a real neighborhood. It was cold that morning so after they dropped us off, they went back to the hotel. There was a large motor home parked in front of the house that served as the wardrobe area/holding area. The driveway in front of the garage is where the commercial was going to be shot. There was a car set up as a prop with a toolbox next to it. The crew was in the process of setting up the lights, cameras, etc. We were greeted by the 2nd AD [15] and introduce to everyone before being offered breakfast and then escorted to the motor home. Coy had a fitting while I filled out paperwork. (There's always paperwork to be filled out)Everyone was really nice. It wasn't some huge production but you could tell that they knew what they were doing. There were no speaking lines in the commercial for anyone. It was just Coy and another male actor playing his dad. He was working on the car and Coy reaches into the toolbox and brings him a tool. Pretty simple. I had the feeling that this scene was just a small

[15] *2nd AD- The second Assistant Director. This person is responsible for creating the call sheet based on the production schedule as well as coordinating the cast and extras.*

part of what was going to be just a montage of shots about CarQuest. Keisha and Chayse picked us up from the set once we were done. We stopped and had breakfast at IHOP and headed back to Columbia. So here was the tally: We left Columbia at about 6pm on Wednesday and got back at 3pm on Thursday. In total, Coy spent two hours on set, about 30 minutes of that time actually filming, for a grand total of $1,500.00. Not bad. Not bad at all.

12

THE CALL THAT CHANGED IT ALL

While Coy and I were on tour, I thought about and decided that I would get a part-time job at UPS upon my return. I wanted to earn some extra money for the holidays and now to help with our move. I started the application process for UPS towards the end of October. By the time I got through the interview and training process, it was the second week of November. I started work on Monday, November 9, 2009. On Wednesday, Nov. 11, I got a call from John Shea, Coy's agent at Frontier Booking in New York. He said that he had an audition for Coy for a play. The *Miracle Worker* was being cast for a Broadway run and they wanted to see Coy for a role. They felt that he had the right look for the part and liked the fact that he had just finished working on stage. John asked if we would be able to bring Coy to NY for an audition on Monday. I told him that I was pretty sure we could be there but I had to check with Keisha to see about how we would work it out with her job. I told him I'd call him back as soon as I spoke with her.

Now. Here's something you have to understand. My beautiful, lovely wife usually calls me several times a day. Several. Times. A. Day. I called her immediately after hanging up with John. No answer. I called again two minutes later. No answer. Three minutes later. No answer. Two minutes later. No answer. You get the picture. I had the most exciting news to share with the most important person in my life, and I couldn't get in touch with her! I called and called and called. Finally, after about 20 or so minutes of calls, she picked up...

"Is something wrong?"

"No..no." I said. "I just have to talk to you about something. Do you have a minute?"

"I can't right now. I'm doing a phone interview. I'll call you back when I'm done."

"Keisha." I said. "Call me **as soon as** you get done!"

"Ok. I will."

"Keisha!" I said. "As soon as you get done!"

"Ok Derek, I will! Bye!"

So my exciting news would have to wait.

A couple of hours later, I picked Coy up from school and decided to have some fun with him. I wasn't going to tell him about the audition because I wanted Keisha and I to tell him together. But I had to do something with this big news, right? When he and his friend got in the truck, I started asking Coy questions about Helen Keller. It was funny because he was talking to his friend and I kept interrupting with questions.

"Coy, have you ever heard of Helen Keller?"

"Yeah."

"Who was she?"

"She was blind or something."

"Did you learn about her in school?"

"Yeah."

"When?"

"I don't know Dad, in fourth grade I think."

"Was she a real person?"

"Daaaad! I don't remember. Why are you asking me so many questions about Helen Keller??"

"Just curious. I saw something on television about her."

I love messing with my children. So much fun. Little did he know, there was a reason for my madness!

Keisha finally called me a little while later and I told her the good news. She was just as excited as I was. I told her that the audition was on Monday but I thought that we should prepare to stay for the entire week, just in case he got a callback and they wanted to see him again a couple of days later. She agreed and said that getting off work for the week would be no problem. She had some vacation days left and she would just use those. Financially, it was going to be even tougher than usual because we really didn't have the money to stay at a hotel in the city for a week. Looking for a solution, Keisha called an aunt that lives in Brooklyn. She explained the situation to her and how long we wanted to stay. Fortunately for us, her Aunt Janie welcomed us into her home. That really helped us out because we wouldn't have been able to stay as long we needed to. Coy's school wasn't an issue. As I mentioned earlier, Heathwood Hall was very supportive of him. They knew that he was acting so when I told them that we had to take him out for a week to audition for a Broadway play, they were more than happy to excuse him. We simply did it the same way we did when he was doing *Raisin*. They would just e-mail me Coy's assignments and homework and we would do it and I'd send it back.

Although I had literally just started at UPS, taking off of work wasn't going to be a problem for me either. I went to my supervisor the next day and simply explained to him what the situation was. I told him that I had every intention of being a reliable employee but this was an opportunity for my son that we couldn't pass up. He understood and told me that it was ok, just come back in to work when I returned. I think the fact that during my short three days there, I had shown them that I was a hard worker and was going to be someone they could depend on helped. The bottom line was, as badly as I needed that job at that time, there was no way that it was going to keep us from taking Coy to New York. Pass up on a chance for a Broadway play to keep an $8.50 an hour seasonal job?? Yeah, right.

Since the audition was on Monday, we decided to travel on Saturday so that Sunday could be just a day to relax. On Friday afternoon, John Shea called again. He said that there was a casting call for a new sitcom for TBS. He said it would be a long shot because they were doing a nationwide search for the roles but since we were going to be in the city anyway, would Coy like to do it? I asked Coy and he said yes so I told John to set it up. He e-mailed me the sides and audition information a couple of hours later. The show was called *Are We There Yet?*. It was based on the Ice Cube movies *Are We There Yet?* and *Are We Done Yet?* We were familiar with both movies and in fact, had them both on DVD. They were great family movies about a single man (Ice Cube) who at first dates, then marries a single mother (played in the movies by Nia Long) of two. When I looked at the audition information, I realized that it was on the same day as The Miracle Worker.

13

NEW YORK, NEW YORK, BIG CITY OF DREAMS

So, once again, we hit I95 North, headed for the Big Apple. This would be the fifth trip up the east coast for me since April and the fourth for the family. We were starting to become very familiar with I-95. It takes approximately 12 hours from Columbia, SC to New York City. Once you get up past the Washington, D.C. area, 95 breaks off into different highways, (295, 395, etc) and then you have the tolls starting around the New Jersey area. Other than that it's not a bad drive. On road trips like this, Keisha and I work really well together. I drive and she handles everything that goes on in the back with Coy and Chayse. Anyone who has traveled with kids know that I have the easier job!

We got to Brooklyn at about midnight that Saturday. On

Sunday, we took the boys into the city to hang out for a while and then returned to the house that afternoon. Coy and I went over his lines for both auditions and for good measure, I called Patrick Malone and had him do a session with Coy over the phone. While he was doing that, I went online and plotted our trip for the next day. Even though we had our vehicle, it's much easier to travel around the city via the subway. We wanted to get the boys in bed early that night because Coy had a big day the next day and we wanted him to be well rested. All was well until about midnight. Chayse woke up vomiting and complaining that his throat was itching. We couldn't figure out what was wrong until Keisha's cousin told us that she had given him a pistachio earlier that night. Little did she know, Chayse has a nut allergy. So while we now knew what the problem was, we were even more concerned at that point and decided to take him to the emergency room. So there we were, 1 o'clock in the morning at the emergency room the night before the biggest auditions in Coy's young career. The doctor confirmed that Chayse was probably having an allergic reaction and gave him some medicine. They wanted him to stay for a while just to monitor him so at about 1:30, Coy and I went back to the apartment so that he could get some sleep. I went back a couple of hours later and picked Keisha and Chayse up. Whew! What a night!

Both auditions were in the afternoon in the vicinity of Times Square so we went early enough to have lunch in the area. The Miracle Worker was first. When we arrived at the audition, there was one other boy waiting with his mother. We signed in and Coy was called back after about 5 minutes. The audition took only another five minutes, and he came walking out of the office. We can always tell how Coy feels about his audition by the look on his face. We've taught him not to worry about what the casting agent or director thinks. The objective is to go in and focus on doing the very best that you can. That's it because that's all you can control. You can't control what they're thinking or what's motivating them to cast this part, so why worry about it? Focus on what you can control, which is your performance. If he doesn't feel that he did his best, he isn't necessarily upset or anything, there is just a distinctive difference in the look he has when he feels like he nailed it.

He came out looking like he felt good about it. He wasn't overly excited, which meant that he probably felt that he could have done better, but he wasn't disappointed either. We asked him how it was and he said, "Good. I think I did good." So that was that. Time to move on to the next one. It was only about four blocks away so we headed in that direction. On the way over, Coy and I went over his lines a couple of times, just to get him in the mind set of this character. Although both roles were for a 10-12 year old African-American boy, they couldn't have been more different. One lived in the late 18th century in Alabama and the other lived in contemporary Seattle, WA.

We got to the location about ten minutes early and there were already three or four other boys there. More would come in while we were there. We signed in and sat down, waiting for Coy to be called in. This office was much smaller than the other place so even though the auditions were taking place in a room with the door closed, we could hear everything that was going on. After two or three other kids had come and gone, Coy's name was called. He got up and headed towards the door. He exchanged greetings with the casting director and headed towards the room. The man noticed that Coy didn't have his script in his hand.

"Hey, I think you forgot your script." he said to Coy.

"Oh, no sir. I don't need it." Coy replied. "I know the lines."

"Oh. Ok." he replied with a surprised look on his face.

Once they started, everyone in the waiting area could hear them. Coy was amazing! It was as if he had been playing that character for years. Being in the waiting area with the other kids and their parents became a little uncomfortable because they were all hearing the same thing we were hearing and they began to look at us as if they were trying to figure out who we were or who he was. He was *that* good. Afterwards, we heard the guy tell him that he was great and wanted to know if he could read some more. Coy said yes and came out to get his script. When he walked out of the room, it was clear that he felt great about it. He walked out, came towards us and was like, "I need my script, he wants to read some more." When he went back in, the tension in the room really amped up. I've never seen some of the nasty looks we were getting! It was funny!

Once it was over, they came out and the casting director shook our hands and told us that he had done a great job. We left feeling great about everything. Coy was SUPER excited. "I nailed it Dad!" This was great simply because he felt like he had done the best he could. I told him that we were proud of him and that no matter what happens, you did your best which is all you can ask for. We left and hung out in Times Square for a while before heading back to Brooklyn.

Because we had decided to stay for the week, we had a few days to kill before heading back on Friday. On Tuesday and Wednesday, we got up, had breakfast, Coy did his school work, and then we headed to the city. We went the Museum of Natural History, Central Park and the Central Park Zoo, just basically hung out in the greatest city in the world for two days. On Thursday we just hung around the house all day. Since we were planning to head back to Columbia on Friday morning, I called John to see if he had heard anything about the *Miracle Worker* audition. See, that's the one we were thinking about. Truth be told, at that point, we really thought that there was no way that a kid from Columbia, SC who had barely been doing this for a year, could end up as a regular cast member on a sitcom on TBS. It just didn't seem possible. Don't get me wrong. I believed that he had what it takes to make it. I just didn't think it could happen that fast. So by Thursday evening, we hadn't really thought about that audition. I called his agent to let him know that we were planning to leave the next day.

"Hey John. How are you?"

"Good. How are you?"

"Good. I just wanted to see if you heard anything about the play and to let you know that we are leaving first thing in the morning."

"Yeah. They said that he did a good job and they really like him, but not for this part. He's too articulate."

"Oh, ok. Well, that's good. As parents, we can live with him being too articulate."

"Yeah, I know right?"

"Ok. Well, we're gonna head back first thing in the morning so let us know if something else comes up."

"Wait, I'm not finished. I was just about to call you. You didn't hear the good news".

"Oh, ok."

"The people from *Are We There Yet?* LOVED him!

"Really?!"

"Yes. They want to see him again. Probably sometime after the Thanksgiving holiday. I was waiting to hear from them today about a date which is why I hadn't called yet."

"Wow. Ok. So just let us know when and we'll bring him back up here."

I hung up the phone and shared the news with the family. We were ecstatic to say the least. It was a little weird for me because this exciting news could mean everything, but at the same time, it could turn out to be nothing. It was hard not to be excited but I reminded everyone that this was just the first step. Coy still had another audition and possibly another after that.

Let's just stay focused.

We got on the road the next morning for what would be the shortest 12 hour drive I've ever taken. My mind was all over the place! I kept trying to figure out (even though there was no way I could possibly know) how close Coy was to getting the part. How many other kids had gotten callbacks? 10? 20? 5? Where was he at on their list in terms of who they liked the most so far? At the top? In the middle? At the bottom? What was going to be the deciding factor? Could he possibly do better than he had done in his first audition? Was there a kid who had been better? Would they change their mind about the callback altogether? These are just a few of the things that were going through my mind during the drive back.

I also thought about what would happen if he got the part. Like, if he actually *got the part*. Our whole lives would change. Now, a lot of people might think that when I say that our whole lives would change, I'm talking in terms of our finances. But nothing could be further from the truth. I had no idea what kind of salary Coy would be making if he got the part so any thought of it would have been pure speculation. No. I was talking about our day to day lives. First of all, we would have to move because the show was being filmed in Stamford, CT. But even deeper than that, I was talking about the world in which we lived would be different. What I mean is, in Columbia, we would get up in the morning, Keisha would go to work, I would take Coy and Chayse to school, pick them up, go to class myself, come home, eat, go to the Y and do my basketball training, etc. We had a typically "normal" life. But if he got this job, all of that would change. And at the time, I wasn't really sure exactly how. I just knew that things would be drastically different. We would be spending most of our time on a soundstage, even though I didn't really know what that entailed. We would all of a sudden be thrust into a world that, up to that point, I had only seen on television and read about in magazines. Interviews and red carpet events. SAG and WGA strikes would all of a sudden be relevant. Thinking of all of this made me crazy! Then I thought, "How can I be thinking of all of this when he'd only gotten a callback??" Then again, how could I not?

14

I-95...AGAIN

We got home late Friday night and tried our best to just live everyday as normal as possible. Thanksgiving was the next week so that gave us something to look forward to. John said that they would want to see us after Thanksgiving so I didn't expect to hear from him before then. We ended up spending Thanksgiving in Augusta, GA with some good friends. Earlier, I mentioned us going to an NBA game at Madison Square Garden to see our friend Mike Curry. He and his wife Katrina are two of our best friends going way back to our college years. They are our boys' Godparents and have four kids of their own ranging in age from 25-17. Mike is a former professional basketball player as well. He started his career in Europe and ended up playing several years in the NBA before moving on to a coaching career.

During our playing years, we had the same agent and trainer and worked out together in the off season. He was a mentor to me and helped me out on and off the court in more ways than he probably knows. Our families are very close, often spending vacations and holidays together. They are about three years older than we are and have always been very supportive of us and our family. We had a great day with them and then spent a quiet, normal weekend at home. On Sunday night, I told Keisha that I expected to hear from John the next day. It was almost December and the show was scheduled to start production in January. I thought that they would want to cast the roles as soon as possible.

Sure enough, at about 10am Monday morning, John called me. I was back at work at UPS so he left a message. He said that they wanted to see us on Friday at 2. There would be other girls and boys there who were up for the roles of the sister and brother on the show. They would be mixed and matched and do some scenes together so that the producers could get a feel for chemistry. So there it was. We would embark on yet another trip to New York. I wanted Coy to be well rested so I decided to leave on Wednesday and use that as a travel day. That way he would have all day Thursday to relax and prepare.

The next day, I approached my supervisor at UPS. I explained the situation to him and told him that I had to leave again. He said that he fully understood my dilemma but that if I left again, he would not be able to keep me on. I told him that I fully understood *his* position but there was no way that I was *not* going. He understood and told me that I could finish out the day, so I did. At the end of my shift, I punched out and that was the end of my career at UPS. At total of ten days! My training lasted longer than that! We got up early Wednesday morning and hit I-95...again.

Since we were only staying for three days, we were able to get a hotel room. This time we stayed in Queens. On Thursday, we got up and started to get dressed to go out for a while. John called to tell us that he had gotten Coy an audition for *Law and Order* the next morning. He also told us that the people from

Are We There Yet? called and said that they had changed their minds about what they wanted to do on Friday. There would be no reading with other kids. They just wanted to meet us. Period. Keisha and Coy asked me what that meant. Was it good or bad? I told them that it was a great thing! Producers will often meet with the family of a child actor before they are hired for a major role because they will have to deal with that family on a regular basis and they want to be sure that the parents aren't crazy. We all started jumping around and screaming! Then, I broke it all up by saying,

"By the way, you've got an audition for *Law and Order* in the morning as well."

More jumping and screaming. (Our family loves *L&O*).

On Friday morning, we headed to the city for Coy's *Law and Order* audition. It was at 11 and we had the meeting with the producers of *Are We There Yet?* at 2. As excited as Coy was about meeting the producers, he was just as excited about his *Law and Order* audition. The scene he was doing called for him to cry and he worked on it all day Thursday. He was anxious to actually try it out for real. The audition was at Chelsea Piers in lower Manhattan which, apparently, is where all of the *Law and Order* auditions take place. We waited for Coy, as usual, in the waiting area. When he was done, he came out with a huge smile on his face.

"I did it Dad! I cried!"

"Did you? Nice man. Good job!"

"Yeah. She said that I did a good job."

"Nice! That's what I'm talking about!"

We left and headed back to Times Square. The meeting with the *AWTY* producer was at the same office that Coy had auditioned at. We had lunch in Times Square and then headed to the office, arriving about ten minutes early. The casting director came out and told us that the producer had called and was running about 15 minutes late. He said to apologize to us and that he would be there as soon as possible. About thirty minutes later, the casting director came back out and told us that they had called again to apologize. They were actually coming in from Stamford, CT and there was an accident on I 95. They said that they would be there as soon as they could. At that point, the casting director stayed in the waiting room and hung out with us. (which never happens!) He talked with us, played with Chayse, and even brought his laptop out and showed us Coy's audition tape. All of this was out of character for a casting director and it made me really comfortable with the situation. I felt more and more confident about Coy's chances.

Finally, at about 3:15, the producer walked in with his assistant. Matt Alvarez is a partner at CubeVision, one of the production companies behind the films and the television show. He was really nice and apologetic for being late. (like we were going to leave or something...yeah, right) It was really informal and relaxed. He just asked us a few general questions about the family, had we ever seen the movies, etc. You could tell that they were basically just checking us out. It only lasted for about 10 minutes. (Imagine that. We drove 12 hours for a ten minute meeting. Would you?) We all said our goodbyes and he said that he would be in touch with Coy's agent. We left the meeting feeling really, really good about Coy's chances. You could tell that they really liked him but we knew that nothing was final until we got the official word. John called a couple of hours later to tell us that they said they would be in touch and that he would call me as soon as he heard anything. We headed back to SC on Saturday morning to begin the long process of...waiting.

15

THE WAITING GAME

I woke up Monday morning as anxious as I had ever been in my entire life. I knew that the call could come at any time. Every time my phone rang, my heart would start pounding in my chest. I would grab my phone and look at the number, hoping it would be a 212 area code. I mean, they called the first thing Monday morning the week before, right? All day. Every time my phone rang. All. Day. Can you imagine? It was like the world had come to a standstill. I couldn't focus on anything else. My son might actually get this part and be a regular cast member on a sitcom. How could I focus on anything else?

Monday came and went without incident. I woke up on Tuesday and it was the same thing. All day. Every time my phone rang. I was driving myself nuts! I tried to keep myself busy but I couldn't. My mind kept drifting back to it. What were they doing? Why was it taking so long to call? Were they still auditioning people? Were they trying to decide between Coy and someone else? Had they changed their minds altogether? This was unusual for me because I am usually better at handling things like this. I tend to do a good job of not worrying about things that I have no control over(a category under which this particular situation definitely fell). But this was somehow different. Maybe because it was my son and not me. I don't know. Coy didn't seem particularly anxious about it. When I picked him up from school on Monday and Tuesday, he asked if I'd heard anything from John, but that was about it. Keisha would call on occasion and ask me if I had heard anything.

By Wednesday, I had almost lost my mind. I wanted to call John but I thought, "He said he would call when he heard something so calling him kind of doesn't make any sense." Keisha called me at some point and I jokingly said that she should stop calling me because every time my phone rings, my heart is about to jump out of my chest. The day went by, again, with no phone call. On

Thursday morning, I woke up feeling a lot more relaxed for some reason. I got up and went through my normal routine. Keisha called me at about 10. I talked with her for a few minutes and then she said, "I guess you haven't heard anything, huh?" It was then that I realized that I hadn't thought about it all day. I didn't even think about it when the phone rang from her call. So at this point, things were getting back to normal. Thursday was just a regular day.

That evening at around 5:30, I was in the kitchen cooking dinner. Keisha was playing with the boys. They were running around the house, screaming and chasing each other. My phone rang and I went and picked it up to see who it was, not thinking at all about the tv show. I looked at the number, and noticed that it had a 212 area code. It was John!. My heart started pounding! Keisha and the boys happened to be right at the kitchen door at the time. I yelled, "Hold on! Hold On! It's John!" They literally froze, right where they were.

"Hello?"

"Hey." he said.

"Hey John. I replied. "How are you?

"I'm good, how are you guys?" he said.

"We're good." I said.

"Couple of questions. "he said." Coy is 11 and will be twelve in June, correct?"

"Right." I replied.

"Ok. That's what I thought." He responded. "And he's now in the 6th or 7th grade?"

"He's in the 6th grade."

"Alright. He replied. "Gotcha. That's all I needed. Thanks."

"Wait, wait! I said. "Have you heard anything about the show."

"You mean *Are We There Yet?*" he asked.

"Yeah." I replied.

"Of course." He said. "I've been working on the contract since Tuesday. Didn't I call you?"

"What!? No! He got it!?

"Yeah. They called on Monday to offer him the part. They faxed the contract over on Tuesday. I'm sorry,

I thought I called you guys."

"No! We've been waiting to hear from you all week!

"I'm so sorry!"

By now, I had given the rest of the family the thumbs up and they were running around the house screaming. When I got off the phone, we all gathered in the kitchen. Coy was thanking God over and over. We had family prayer and just thanked God for the opportunity.

Wow. It took a while for the news to sink in. It was kind of surreal. That night, I lay in bed thinking about the journey we had been on for the past year. Orlando. New York. New York again. And again. And again. Vermont. LA. New York again. Past due bills. Water and electricity turned off. Then on. Then off again. It had been a tough couple of years but now a whole new world of opportunity was about to be opened up to us. It was crazy because for the last 2 or 3 years before all of this, I use to say to Keisha all the time, "I feel like something big is coming." That was all I could say. I couldn't put it into words but I felt like something big was going to happen to us that would change our lives. I didn't know what it was or when it was coming, but there was no doubt in my mind that it was coming.

The next day, we began spreading the good news to friends and family. Everyone was happy and excited for us. A few days later, John sent the contract over for us to look over and sign. The show would be filmed in Stamford, CT over a period of five weeks. They would put us up in a hotel for the duration of the shoot. The production company had a 10 episode (essentially a pilot[16]) deal with TBS, who had an option for 90 more episodes after the initial 10 ran on air. The first week would consist of table reads and rehearsals. Then they would shoot two episodes per week during the second and third weeks, and three episodes per week during the last two weeks. The deal was a result of the success that TBS has had with its Tyler Perry shows, *House of Payne* and *Meet the Browns*, both of which received large episode orders. Production was scheduled to begin in January. So now, the plans to move to LA were put on hold. Keisha took another leave of absence from her job so that we

---

[16] *Pilot-The first taped episode of a television show. It is used to determine whether or not the proposed show is marketable.*

could all be together. This was a hug step for Coy and the entire family and we all wanted to do it together.

One issue that we had to deal with in light of the circumstances was school. Coy was of course still enrolled at Heathwood Hall and they had been very cooperative and flexible in working with us up to this point. But to ask for another 5 weeks was a bit much to say the least. There would be a tutor on set for Coy and the young lady who played his sister. They would be required to do 15 hours of school per week. I did some research and found a couple of home school programs that cater to the needs of children who are not traditional students due to their particular lifestyle. Keisha and I discussed it and thought that it would be easier for Coy and his onset tutor if he started fresh with a whole new homeschool program that was flexible enough to accommodate his needs. Also, once the filming was complete and we returned to Columbia, I could continue the program with him. So, he would finish out the semester at Heathwood and I enrolled him in the online homeschool program to begin after the Christmas break.

16

ARE WE THERE YET

Coy was scheduled to report to Stamford on Monday, January 11th. The cast wouldn't arrive until that Tuesday but he had to start school. We left late Saturday night and hit I-95 yet again, this time, headed to Connecticut. We arrived Sunday morning and checked into our hotel. The Holiday Inn Downtown Stamford would be "home" for the next five weeks. Just another stop on the journey. On Monday, we took Coy to the studio and met just about everyone involved with the show with the exception of the rest of the cast. The writers, producers, director, production assistants, etc. We met Coy's teacher and co-star who would be playing his sister. While Coy did school, Keisha, Chayse, and I just hung out around the production office talking and getting to know people. It was all exciting and somehow normal at the same time. Like, the production office was much like any other work atmosphere

you might walk into. There were people at desks with laptops

working, answering phones. There were dry erase boards and

calendars on the walls. The only difference was that the phone

calls might be about casting calls for extras and the dry erase

boards had episode information. It was all pretty typical. Except

it wasn't typical. Not to us anyway. It was pretty cool. As I

mentioned earlier, I have always been a big movie and

television buff. Never really interested in being in front of the

camera but extremely interested in what was going on behind

it. Now, I was about to find out first hand.

The studio is located in a two story building that also houses

another company. The production offices are on the second

floor and the soundstage is in the back of the building on the

first floor. We got a chance to go down to the set on that first

day which was amazing. It really hit me then that Coy was going

to be on television. Wow.

The next day was the first table read and the day we met the rest of the cast. Terry Crews would play Nick, the stepdad. Essence Atkins would play Suzanne, the mom. Keesha Sharp would play Gigi, Suzanne's best friend. And comedian Christian Finnegan would play Martin, Nick's best friend. There would also be recurring appearances by executive producer Ice Cube, who plays Suzanne's brother Terrance, the wonderful Telma Hopkins, who plays Nick's mother, and Michael D'Darrio who plays Kevin's best friend. During the table read, they read five of the ten episodes that they were going to shoot. Afterwards, Coy did a couple of hours of school and then we headed back to the hotel.

Wednesday and Thursday was pretty much the same. Coy had a couple of wardrobe fittings, they had table reads, and school. Not necessarily in that order. On Friday, they had their first full rehearsal. This is when they would actually be on set, walking through each scene, feeling out the movements, working on camera positions, etc. This was really cool because we got to see how it all comes together. Just like with the movie *Nailed*, I had no idea that it took so many people to make a television show. They went through all of the scenes of the two episodes that they were going to shoot the next week. Coy also did more school.

Monday was the first day of shooting and by the time we got to the studio, I was a nervous wreck! You'd think that by this point, I would have figured out that Coy is going to be just fine. I've never seen him that excited. After breakfast at the studio, he got dressed, went to hair and makeup, and we headed down to the set. I have to admit, it was pretty exciting. It was still kind of surreal. The fact that he was already doing this still kind of blows me away. He walked on set like he had been doing it his whole life, greeting everyone from Terry Crews, the star of the show, to the catering people along the way. His comfort level and excitement relaxed me a lot. I finally figured that if he wasn't nervous, why should I be?

As the days went by, we got more and more comfortable and sort of got into a groove. They would send a driver to pick Coy and me up every morning. His call times varied, anywhere from

7:15-9:30am. Once we got to the studio we would have breakfast and then he would change into whatever outfit they had waiting for him in his dressing room, go to hair and makeup, and then either go to school or straight to set. His dressing room was located on the same level as the production office, near the room they used for school. A typical day might go like this:

7:00am-Wake Up

7:45am-Van Pick up in front of the hotel

8:00-8:45am- Eat breakfast at the studio, hair and make up.

8:45-9:30am- School

9:30am-11:30-On set filming

11:30-1:00- School

1:00-2:00 On set filming

2:00-3:00 Lunch

3:00-3:15 Hair and makeup touch up

3:15-4:30 On Set filming

4:30-5:30 School

5:30 End of day

This is just an example of what a day might look like. The times will vary but it's pretty much what he would do Monday through Thursday. On Friday, they would rehearse the episodes that they were shooting the following week. Keisha and Chayse would come to the studio from time to time as well. They would rarely spend the entire day there because Chayse was only three at the time and it's difficult for a kid that age to sit around quietly on a set for 8 hours.

It was a wonderful experience for Coy. As a young, inexperienced actor, he got the incredible opportunity to work with people who have been in the business for years. Telma, Essence, Terry, and Keesha all have years and years of sitcom experience and they were all really nice and open. They were very willing to share their knowledge and experience with Coy. Ice Cube even gave him pointers from time to time. Ali Leroi who is the award winning writer/director/executive producer /show runner of the hugely successful sitcom, *Everybody Hates Chris* was also amazing to work with. It was fun watching him on set, down on one knee, explaining to Coy what his motivation was for a particular scene, and then allowing him to figure out how to deliver the line instead of telling him how to say it.

.

Another good thing about working on this sitcom is the speed at which they work. Traditionally, it takes approximately 4-5 days to produce one episode of a sitcom. They have table reads on Mondays and Tuesdays, rehearse on Wednesdays and Thursdays, and then shoot on Fridays. On this show, they were shooting three episodes Mon-Thu! This was a good thing for Coy because, as Terry Crews explained it to me, when he moves on to his next thing, whether it's a movie or another sitcom, the pace is so much slower that it's going to be a breeze for Coy. On this show, he would have to learn three episodes worth of dialogue within 4 days. The thing is, this was his first show so to him, this is how it's suppose to be. He didn't know any different so he was being trained to be better than the typical actor in a lot of ways.

17

I HAVE AN IDEA

As Coy settled in to what he was doing, I started to think about my role in all of this. My job was (and is) a little more involved than most people think. I've had friends say to me..."Man, you've got it made. All you have to do is sit around all day and do nothing." Well, not really. See, I think that parents of child entertainers have gotten a bad rap in general. The impression is that we're either out spending all of our kids' money or sitting around doing nothing. All while our child slaves in front of the camera. I can't speak for everyone but nothing could be further from the truth for us.

See, what people fail to realize, it seems, is that in spite of the fact that our kids are on television, making movies, touring, on the cover of magazines and chatting with talk show hosts, they are still just kids. There is only so much they can do. They can't read and understand contracts, pay union dues and commission fees, rent apartments, fly alone, maintain tax records, etc. All of this and more becomes the job of the parent. And believe me, it is a job. Now there are some who choose to hire business managers to take care of all of these things. The problem for Keisha and me is, business managers cost money. When this is all said and done and Coy comes to us in five years looking for what he's earned, we want to feel good about what he has and know that we did everything we could to protect him and what he's earned.

So to that end, I decided that I had to figure out a way to make a living. It was obviously impossible to hold a regular 9 to 5 so I started thinking about how I could do it while sitting at the studio all day. Sound crazy? Well, it's not as crazy as it may seem. As I said before, it takes a multitude of people to create a television show or movie. We only see the actors and on occasion, the directors. But there are a variety of jobs in the industry that take place off camera. You have camera operators, wardrobe department, carpenters, sound department, editors, set decorators, hair and makeup, the list goes on and on. The one that interested me the most...writing.

Although it may seem like it, this idea isn't completely out of left field. I have always loved to write. During my professional basketball years in Europe, I kept a daily journal simply because I loved to write. I have dozens of composition notebooks filled with stories that I've written over the years, just because. Back in 2007, I enrolled in a local college in Columbia to complete my bachelors degree. I had to take a Math and English placement exam and the English portion was a three page essay. When I called a week later to get my scores, I was told that the professor who graded the English portion of my exam said that it was the best essay he'd read in his 17 years at the college. A couple of semesters later, I had to write a 20 page paper for a history class. Upon reading the paper, my professor, (a thrice published author himself), said that it was one of the best papers he'd read in his 30 years of teaching. He said that I had a knack for storytelling and that I should consider writing something for publication. These compliments were flattering but at the time, I was focused on my basketball training company. Writing wasn't something that I ever considered doing for a living.

As said earlier, I have always loved television and movies. Years ago, before Coy ever thought about acting, I was downloading screenplays off of the internet and reading them for fun. It made sense to me that while I was just sitting on set all day five days a week, I could be learning how to write screenplays. I could take some of the stories that I had written over the years, turn them into screenplays, and attempt to sell them.

Now, I know that some of you are thinking to yourselves, "This guy is crazy." But take a second and think about it... you're reading a book that I've written right now. See? Not so crazy after all, right? I had read about the stories of Sylvester Stallone with Rocky and Ben Affleck and Matt Damon with Good Will Hunting. They were unknowns who wrote and sold screenplays, and later acted in the movies when they were produced. I had no desire to act, but I could definitely write. Also, I could write something for Coy just as Stallone, Affleck, and Damon wrote things for themselves. Remember earlier I mentioned getting to the worst case scenario? Worst case scenario in this situation: I never sell a screenplay. No loss. At least I will have spent my time on set being productive, trying to accomplish something.

So, I now had a purpose. A goal to work towards. I went to a book store and bought several books written by successful screenwriters, on how to write screenplays. Now instead of just sitting on set all day surfing the net and watching movies, I was being productive. It felt good. Great, actually. I had a conversation with Keisha and explained to her what my thought process was now. For all intensive purposes, we are now in the entertainment business. Yes, Coy may be the actor, but because he is a minor and we have to be with him, our entire family is in the business. We have to adjust to our new situation and find a way to make a living in the entertainment business. Like I said earlier, there are more ways to do that than standing in front of a camera.

Before we ever got into this, my curiosity about the industry led to many late night internet surfing sessions over the years. It's amazing what you can find out on the internet. There are many industry inspired websites that have all kinds of information about the entertainment business that the general public doesn't know. The information isn't secret; it's just not stuff that gets reported on Entertainment Tonight. For example, aintitcool.com (Ain't It Cool News) is a website that has information about what movies are going into production, scripts, casting information, possible release dates, etc., all before any of it is officially reported. This information comes from production assistants, secretaries, and other people who work at the studios and production companies.

Finding this kind of information on the internet gave me a pretty good understanding of how the Hollywood machine works. I am speaking specifically about how movies and television shows get made. I also discovered something else that I never knew and that a lot of people I know don't realize. Many actors in Hollywood own their own production companies. This ownership gives them more control over what films they do because it gives them the ability to create projects. Many times, they are producing projects that they aren't even starring in.

This information all of a sudden became relevant to me. After realizing that it would be in Coy's best interest to incorporate him for tax purposes, I thought; why not take it all the way? Why not start a production company, setting us up to be able to create projects in the future? The plan is to write something with Coy attached as the lead, sell it, and try to get our production company involved on the production end. It could be the start of something big. Look, the way I see it, you have to think big to be big. We're in it now so why not? Three years ago, we were living in Columbia, SC and Coy was a student at Lake Carolina Elementary. Now he was a regular on a sitcom on TBS. Anything is possible.

18

TIME FOR A CHANGE

Now that I had a purpose again, I felt a new level of excitement. As always, I prayed about it and felt really good about the direction we were heading in. Throughout this whole experience, I've always maintained my relationship with God through prayer. It really gives me a sense of comfort and confidence. To that end, as time went on, I started to think about what was next for us. I had accepted the fact that we were now in the entertainment business and had a plan for earning a living and being successful within that. Once I made that transition in my mind, Columbia, SC didn't feel right anymore. In fact, as each day went by, I became more and more removed from the idea of going back and living there after the ten episode shoot was over. I had nothing against the city, it just didn't make sense to me to be there anymore in light of the direction our life was heading.

We were scheduled to be done in Stamford around the end of February. The show would air in June and we wouldn't know until July or August if TBS would pick up the 90 episode option. If they did, we would move to Stamford, if not, we were right back at square one. So once we were done filming the ten episodes, Coy would be out of a job with no indication of when he would work again. I felt like we needed to continue to actively pursue this and we couldn't do that in Columbia. We were basically at the same point we were at back in October when we were done with A Raisin in The Sun and had started making preparations to move out west. I still felt very strongly that LA was where we needed to be and thought that we should resume the plan to head out there once we returned to Columbia. At this point, Coy was already in a homeschool program so school was not an issue. We could get an apartment or an extended stay hotel room and spend a couple of months out there letting Coy audition and find his next project. If we were going to be in the entertainment business, we needed to be where the entertainment business was. Bottom line: he has

a better chance of getting a job in LA than he does in Columbia.

The issue with heading out after we were done with the ten

episodes was that it wouldn't have made sense for Keisha to

transfer her job because we didn't really know how long we

were going to be there. Plus, there was a real possibility that we

would be moving to Stamford at the end of the summer

anyway. There were no more vacation days and leaves of

absence left. It was time to start a new chapter in our life and in

order to do this, she would have to leave her job...permanently.

The first time I brought it up to her, she was very skeptical. She

couldn't see herself leaving her job, which at the time was our

main source of income. It's not that she was against going to LA,

she was very supportive of the idea. It's just that for the couple

of years before this, she had been the primary breadwinner for

our family. She felt that it was her responsibility to make sure

that we at least had her salary coming in every two weeks. I

tried to explain to her that while I understood that, I really felt

like it was time for our lives to change. Time for us to take a different path. Sometimes, that can be scary but we couldn't let fear stop us from trying to move forward.

She asked me a lot of questions: What are we going to do about the house? Where are we going to stay when we get out there? How much is it going to cost? What do we do at the end of the two months? What if this show doesn't get picked up? What do we do then? I had answers for some of the questions. I gave her a cost analysis based on flight, hotel, and rental car information I had already looked up. For the other questions, all I could tell her was that I didn't know exactly, but it was all going to work out. She suggested that maybe Coy and I go for a month while she and Chayse stay in Columbia and she continues to work. Coy didn't like this at all. He was excited about the idea of going, but said that it had to be all of us or nothing. He didn't want us to be separated again.

A week or so went by after our initial conversation. I could tell that Keisha wanted to do it, but felt like she couldn't. One day, a few days before we were scheduled to head back to Columbia, one of the producers approached me. He said that he just wanted to mention that they would be bringing us out to LA around the last week of March for about 4 days to shoot promos for the show. This was great news in my mind! When I got back to the hotel that night, I told Keisha. She couldn't understand why I was so excited. I told her that I believed that this was a sign. I was just telling her last week that we should go to LA. Now a producer was telling me that we had to go to LA! I mean, the writing was on the wall, right? Well, she didn't exactly see it the way I saw it. This new development did nothing to convince her that she should quit her job and head west.

The time finally came for us to head back south. We said our goodbye's and promised to keep in touch with everyone (you know, the usual), packed up the Navigator, and hit 95...again! Regardless of whether or not the show would get picked up, I left feeling like it had been a great experience for all of us. We had learned SO MUCH about the industry in the short 5 weeks we were there and Coy had gotten better and better as an actor. I felt really good about where we were. More

importantly, I was excited about where we were going.

19

HEY YOU GUUUYYYYY'S!!

We got home around the last week of February and were scheduled to fly out to LA on March 21, which gave us about a month. Keisha went back to work. I took care of the boys all day, homeschooling Coy. I told her a couple of days after we got there that after much thought and prayer, I thought that we should get the house ready to be vacated when we left in a month. We had already started the process when we had decided to move to LA before Coy got the sitcom. There wasn't much left to do.

We needed to get a few of the rooms painted and continue packing and getting rid of stuff that we didn't want. I told her that whatever God wanted us to do with the house would be done by the 21st. If he wanted us to sell it, we would get an offer by then. If he wanted us to rent it out, we would have tenants by then. It was as simple as that and there was no doubt in my mind that one or the other would happen.

From the date that we got home, Keisha had approximately two weeks to put in her notice at work that she was leaving. I told her that she should let her boss know that she was leaving but decided that I wasn't going to pressure her. Every day she came home, I would just ask her once, "Did you tell her?" Every day, there was another excuse. "I couldn't, she was in meetings all day." "I couldn't, I was swamped with work." "I went into her office to tell her but we started talking about something else and I forgot." Thinking about it now, it's kind of funny! I understood what she was going through. She was having a hard time with it. She was concerned about our finances and knew that once she left her job that was it. I didn't expect her to be where I was in terms of my faith about our future. I was giving her time to come around but at the same time, I was continuing to prepare us for the move. Every day she came home from work, the house was a little more empty. I had no doubts. I didn't know exactly what was going to happen but I knew we were going to be alright.

We were home for a week and then the following weekend, we had to take a trip to Orlando, Fl. It was time for the Talent Inc. Showcase again and Scott Cooper had called to see if Coy would come down and speak. It had been exactly one year since Coy participated in the showcase and Scott thought it would be great for him to share his experiences in the industry since then. Coy of course said yes and we thought it would be a nice vacation after 5 weeks of winter in Connecticut. So on that Friday, we jumped on I- 95 (yes...again!) and headed to Orlando. We went to watch some of the competition on Friday night and that's when it really hit me. That's when I truly realized just how fortunate we were and how much had happened in the last year. It was a surreal feeling and I just remember being so thankful at that moment.

On Saturday morning, we took the boys to Disney World. The weather was beautiful and we had a good time. Coy spoke at the showcase that night and did a great job. I know he's my son and I'm probably more than a little biased but sometimes, the kid really amazes me. He got up on the stage in front of all those people, at the age of 11, and talked about everything he had been through the past year. He encouraged the kids to never stop believing in themselves and the parents to do what they could to support their kids' dreams. You would've thought that he gave motivational speeches for a living. On Sunday morning, we headed back to Columbia and got back to the process of preparing to head out west.

Finally, the day came. It was Friday, March 5th. Two weeks to the day of what would be her last day of work. That morning when she got up for work, I told her that this was it. She had no choice but to do it today. I could tell that she was still uneasy but she knew she had to do it. When she got home that afternoon, she walked in and made the announcement..."I did it." I wasn't surprised because I knew it was inevitable. Coy was jumping around, excited. Which made Chayse jump around excited as well. (although he didn't know why he was excited)

That night, as we lay in bed, she said to me as she turned over to go to sleep. "Well, Mr. Stewart, I did it. I hope you know what you're doing." I believed I did.

Into the next week, we continued to get the house ready to be vacated. We also had a couple of realtors come out and discuss putting the house up for sale. Clearly at that time, we were not in a seller's market. Had we put the house on the market and sold it at that time, we would've taken a huge loss. So, we decided to rent it out instead. We figured if we could rent it out for the amount our mortgage payment was every month, that would be one less bill and we could revisit the issue in a year.

On Friday, March 12th, nine days before we were scheduled to leave for LA, I called three different property management companies and set up appointments for Monday and Tuesday. After meeting with all of them, we decided to go with one and signed a management agreement. On Wednesday, someone from the company came out and took pictures of our home to put on their website. By Thursday afternoon, they had 5 people interested. By Friday, they were showing the house to potential renters. By the time we left on Sunday, we had two different people who wanted to rent! Just like that! Now if that's not a sign that we were heading in the right direction, I don't know what would have been!

In the middle of all of this, there was something else amazing going on. On Monday of the previous week, John Shea called and said that *The Electric Company* was interested in Coy for a role on their show. *The Electric Company*, as many of you know, is a wonderful educational show that people of my generation grew up watching on PBS. The Sesame Workshop decided to bring it back a couple of years ago and was interested in Coy for the third season. They wanted us to put him on tape, so we did. The following week during all of the property management meetings and house showings, we got another call from John. They loved Coy's audition tape and wanted to see him for an audition in person. They knew that we were leaving for LA in a few days and wanted to know if it was possible to bring Coy up to New York before we left. I asked him when...he said on

Friday...I said, "We'll be there."

There are some things are no-brainers. While things were still tight financially, (we basically had what Coy had made for the ten episodes of *Are We There Yet*, which after taxes and commission wasn't a whole lot), there are some things that you just have to do. I wasn't sure that he'd get the job if we went. But the one thing I *was* sure of...he wouldn't get it if we didn't. So...we went. I bought two round trip airline tickets on that day (Thursday) for Friday morning. We were leaving for LA on Sunday so we had to go and come back on the same day. We left the airport in Charlotte at 7am and were back home in Columbia by 12:30 that night. It may seem kind of crazy now, doing that in the middle of moving out of our house and getting ready to head west for an indefinite amount of time. But, if you're going to do something, do it. Coy was an actor. Actor's go on auditions when they have the opportunity.

Coy and I got to New York at around 10. His audition wasn't until that afternoon so we had some time to kill. We had lunch with two of Coy's cast members from *A Raisin in The Sun* who live in New York. Afterwards, we headed uptown. The audition was at the Sesame Workshop offices on 63rd and Broadway. Being in the office with all of the *Sesame Street* memorabilia was kind of cool for me. I grew up watching *Sesame Street* and *The Electric Company* so the idea that my son might have an opportunity to work here was unbelievable. The audition took about 10 minutes. When Coy came back out they told me that he had done a great job and they would be in touch. At that point, we had about three hours to kill before it was time to head to the airport. Turns out, there was a movie theater right there at Lincoln Square so we decided to catch a movie. Once it was over, we took the train out to JFK and headed home.

We got back to Columbia at about 2 am. I was up at 6 Saturday morning because I still had stuff to do at the house. I had to load all of the furniture that we were keeping onto a Uhaul truck, take it to a storage facility, and unload it. The property management company was going to have someone come out and clean the house before our tenants moved in but we still had to get everything out. It was a loooong day to say the least.

On Sunday morning at 5am, a car service arranged by TBS picked us up at our house. As we rode away, I looked back at our home of 7 years. There was a little sadness, but mostly excitement. Sadness because, well, that was our home. It's where we had spent Christmas, New Years, birthdays, and other memorable occasions for the last 7 years. It's where we raised our family and now, we were leaving. Yeah, we would be back in Columbia at some point, but we weren't coming back to this house for who knows how long. But that was the exciting part. Our family was embarking on a new journey. I didn't know where this journey was going to take us, but I was definitely looking forward to the ride.

20

TINSELTOWN

When we got to LA, there was a driver in an SUV waiting to take us to the hotel. They had us staying at the Four Seasons in Beverly Hills. I'm sure that I don't have to explain how nice it was. We were scheduled to be there until Thursday while Coy shot promos for the show. We checked in and then went to the restaurant and got something to eat. Once we got back to the room, we all just crashed. It was quite possibly the best sleep I've ever had. I didn't realize how exhausted we were. We had done SO MUCH the past few days trying to get ready to leave for an indefinite amount of time. Not to mention the trip to New York that Coy and I had taken just 48 hrs before. We slept for about 5 hours in the middle of the day, woke up, raided the mini bar in the room, and then went back to sleep for the night.

The next morning, Coy and I were picked up and taken to the
set. The shoot was at Culver City studios and it was the first
time in all of this that we were on an actual studio lot. We got
there and were greeted by someone from TBS. She was one of
the ladies that was in charge of the promo shoot. We were
escorted to Coy's trailer where we had breakfast before Coy
changed into his wardrobe for the shoot. Hair and make-up was
next which is where we reconnected with the cast. It was good
to see everyone again. The director came in and introduced
himself shortly after we arrived. He was not the same director
who directed the 10 episodes, but was hired to direct the
promos. He gave the cast a rundown of what they would be
doing the next couple of days and what they were looking for
out of the promos. Monday, Tuesday, and Wednesday, was
spent shooting promotional ads for the show that would run on
TBS and TNT during the NBA playoffs. They would begin about a
month and a half before the show was to air. These ads were
scripted "scenes" that had the cast saying and doing things in
character. They also shot sort of a music video, dancing and

singing the theme song of the show. I enjoyed watching it all being done. Now when I watch television and see promos of other shows, I have some idea of what the process of creating them was like. Keisha and Chayse came and spent the day on set on Tuesday. Just like the filming of the episodes, it was too much to ask of him to sit there quietly for hours every day. They spent most of their time hanging out in and around the hotel.

On Thursday, we went to a different location for a photo shoot where they took hundreds of pictures of the cast in character. There were shots of the entire family, individual shots, Coy and Terry, Coy and Essence, Terry and Teala, Coy and Teala, you get the picture. That was a lot of fun. There was upbeat music playing and they all just had a really good time. That afternoon, John Shea called with some good news yet again. Coy had been offered the part in *The Electric Company*! They were going to shoot 12 episodes in Philadelphia in July and August. There was one small issue that needed to be cleared up before we could celebrate. *Are We There Yet?* had first priority in terms of Coy's availability. At that point, they didn't know if the show was going to get picked up or not and if it did, when they would start production again. If it were picked up and they decided to go into production in August, Coy wouldn't be able to do *The Electric Company.* In any case, we would have to get their permission to do it. John didn't think it would be a problem so we didn't worry about it.

After the photo shoot was over, we said our goodbyes to everyone. The ladies from TBS who were in charge of promos asked if we were going to be busy towards the end of May. They said that they were working on something that could further promote the show and asked us to keep the last two weeks in May open if at all possible. I told them that it was no problem. Just let us know when and where and we would be there.

We checked out of the Four Seasons on Friday morning and began what turned out to be a crazy day. We had been invited by one of the executive producers to see an early cut of the first couple of episodes. Coy's manager had also gotten him invited to a red carpet event. But before all of this, we had to check out of the Four Seasons, go to the airport and pick up the rental car that I had reserved, go check into the Residence Inn in El Segundo where we would be staying for the remainder of our time out there, then drive back into downtown LA to the producers office. We had to be at the office by 2 and at the red carpet event at 4. The problem was that the rental car wasn't going to be ready until 12.

By the time we did all of that and made it to the producers' office, it was a little after 2. Everything was ok though because I had called ahead to let him know that we were running behind. I didn't think seeing Coy on television was going to be that big of a deal to me at this point. I mean, I had been on set every day watching them film. What's the difference...right? Wrong!! When the producer put the DVD in and pressed play, I thought I was going to burst! It was the actual show. As if we were watching it on TBS. Credits, show opening, everything. Coy just happened to be in the first scene of the first show and when I saw him on the screen as his name was displayed in the credits, it was unbelievable.

It was just...amazing. I mean, don't get me wrong, I have a pretty good grasp on reality and I know that him being on television doesn't make him better than anyone else. But as I sat there and watched the show, I couldn't help being proud. I thought about the day he told me that he wanted to be an actor. I thought about how difficult it was for him spending the summer in NY without me. I thought about the courage it takes for him to openly say "This is what I want to do.", and then go about the process of doing it, with no fear whatsoever. I thought about Keisha and me. What we had been through and what we each had given up. It was just a really emotional moment for me. We watched a couple of episodes and the producer shared with us some data that he had gotten from some test audiences. It all seemed to be positive. I liked the show and I felt like it was going to do well. Next it was time to head to the red carpet event. It was being held at a club on Hollywood Boulevard which in a city with normal traffic was about 20 minutes from where we were at the time. But this was LA so it took us about 50 minutes. We got there and it was packed!! This was an event for a kids charity so there were plenty of child entertainers everywhere. Kids from Nickelodeon and Disney were running around all over the place. Coy's manager thought it would be good for him to be in that environment to start thinking of charities that he would like to get involved with and to generate some press for himself and the show. We hung out for a little while, Coy did the red carpet and a couple of interviews, and then we left.

That Saturday, the Kids Choice Awards was scheduled to be held at Pauley Pavilion on the campus of UCLA. Coy and I had been invited to attend by someone who happened to have a couple of extra tickets. This was going to be a lot of fun for Coy because he watched the KCA's on television every year and is a big fan of a lot of the actors that were scheduled to be there. While the person who gave us the tickets, a well known celebrity, arrived in front of the crowd in a Cadillac Escalade with a driver, Coy and I drove the Ford Flex that we had rented and parked in the parking garage across the street. I liked that it happened this way because I thought it was important for Coy to get a look at this "celebrity thing" up close, but from the outside. I wanted him to see it for what it really is, and that is -**other people giving you worth and telling you how great you are**- when truly, it is up to us to define who we are. I told him that one day, he might be famous but he had to always remember this time. The time when no one knew who he was and treated him like they would treat anyone else. Because if he ends up becoming "famous", people would start to treat him differently. But it wouldn't be because *he* had changed, it would be because *their perception of him* had changed. I said that if he always remembered this, it would be easy for him to stay grounded. The awards show was great. We had a really good time. We got a chance to walk the "orange carpet" which was crazy but a lot of fun. After the show, there was an after party where we met a lot of cool people, Justin Beiber, George Lopez, David Spade, to name a few. On the way home that night, Coy said that he couldn't believe that the year before, he was watching the KCA's on television and now he had actually been there. He wondered aloud where he would be during next year's show. Good question. The answer remains to be seen.

21

FROM MINT TO LINT

We had made quite the change in location when we left the

Four Seasons and checked into the Residence Inn. Coy said, "I

went from mint on my pillow, to lint on my pillow." Which

Keisha and I thought was hilarious! Don't get me wrong, the

Residence Inn wasn't a bad place. It just wasn't the Four

Seasons. But we were happy to be where we were and happy

that we were all together. The future was bright as far as we

were concerned so there was no reason for us to be anything

but happy!

We spent the first few days just kind of getting settled in and

eventually got into somewhat of a routine. We would get up

every morning and Coy and I would do school. He would have

two, maybe three auditions a week, usually right in LA although he did have a couple in Santa Monica which is just a few miles west. Whenever we went into LA for an audition, we would make a day of it. We'd go to Hollywood Boulevard to the Kodak Theater, Madame Tussauds, or Ripley's Believe It Or Not. We'd hang out at the Beverly Center and The Grove. On the days that he didn't have an audition, we would take the boys to the park in Manhattan Beach or take rides up the Pacific Coast Highway and through Topanga Canyon. I enjoyed the rides because it was a great way to get familiar with the city.

On Thursday afternoons, Coy got a real treat. Patrick Malone had an acting class on Thursday's at his studio, The Actor's Spot, in North Hollywood. Coy had really enjoyed working with him when he came to Columbia to do the acting workshop. We would take him every week and he would have a blast. It was fun for him to take the class and have a chance to work with other kids who were actively going on auditions and working just as he was. Plus, Patrick is really good and Coy has learned a lot from him.

Time went on and we got more and more comfortable with the idea of living out there. For me, LA felt like the land of opportunity. I'm not sure why but being out there made me feel like anything was possible. Like we could have a fresh start and do anything we wanted to do. At that time, our future was uncertain but I had no doubts. I felt very strongly that we were on the right path and would end up exactly where we were supposed to be.

During this time, we also gained some new, very dear friends. We had gotten to know Essence Atkins and her husband Jaime Mendez during our time spent in Stamford. They lived in LA and when they learned that we would be staying out there for a while after the promo shoot, they said that they would have us over to their house at some point. A few days after the *Kids Choice Awards*, Jaime contacted me and said that they were having some people over for the NCAA Final Four and would love for us to come. We had a great time and it was the beginning of what has become a true friendship between them and our family. Not only were they supportive of what we were trying to do for Coy, but it was nice to have someone out there who truly cared about us.

Coy continued to go on auditions, mostly for commercials and print ads. He got a lot of callbacks but never landed anything, just like the previous summer he had spent in New York. It was kind of interesting to witness because it never bothered him. He would get excited when he got an audition, learn his lines and go in and do his best. But it never bothered him that he wasn't booking anything. Part of it was because we always made sure that he didn't feel like the audition was everything. We always planned things to do before and after his auditions so that he got the feeling that the audition was just a part of our day. But more importantly, I think the main reason it never bothered him is because he truly feels like if he doesn't book a particular part, that role wasn't for him. We always tell him that what's for him is for him and no one can deny that when it happens. Every audition is simply preparing him for the next one. He believed this and was never upset when he didn't book a job. It was really interesting to watch such a young kid handle it that way.

One day, we were on our way to an audition when Keisha got a call from one of the ladies from the promo department at TBS. After all the usual pleasantries, she told Keisha that they had set up a radio press junket for the main cast and Ice Cube at Disney World in Orlando. It would be for the weekend and the entire family was invited. The dates were from May 21-23. More great news. Who doesn't like a free trip to Disney World?!

We were scheduled to leave LA on May 9th and return to South Carolina. That gave us two months out there and when I was planning the trip, I thought that was a good amount of time to stay based on our financial situation. Initially upon our return to Columbia, we were going to stay with Keisha's sister in the house that she grew up in. I didn't know how long that was going to be because I had no idea where our next stop was going to be. But now that Coy had booked *The ElectricCompany*, we knew where we would be during the months of July and August. The plan was to head home on the 9th, and spend some time in Columbia before heading down to Myrtle Beach to spend a week with the Curry's. We were going to relax at the

beach and catch the premiere of *Are We There Yet?* with them

on June 2nd. That was the plan anyway. But as we were starting

to learn, in this business, your plans don't mean anything.

22

THE GLADES

Coy had an audition on Monday May 3rd for a guest spot on a new drama that was going to air on A&E in August. On Wednesday, Jamie called and said that he had a callback on Thursday. On Friday morning, two days before we were scheduled to head back to South Carolina, we found out that Coy had book the job. They were filming in Florida in the Miami area and wanted to fly us down on Tuesday for seven days! Crazy! It was just like the previous summer in New York when he spent a month and a half auditioning and booked *A Raisin in the Sun* two days before I was coming to pick them up. So, we flew to Columbia on Sunday, spent Monday unpacking, washing clothes, and packing again, and then flew to Miami on Tuesday. Whew! Normally when dealing with a child actor, the production company will provide two first class airline tickets for the child and a parent. When TBS flew us out to LA, Coy and I flew first class and we purchased two coach tickets for Keisha and Chayse. (To all of the wives reading this: For the record, I insisted that Keisha take the first class ticket and I would travel with Chayse. But she preferred sitting with him.)This time, we asked Jamie if she could get them to just get four coach tickets, which they gladly did.

So here we were. Approximately two years after Coy started taking classes at DeAbreu in Columbia and he had already booked one play, three television shows, and a regional commercial. Pretty good for a kid from South Carolina who just kind of stumbled into acting. The day before we left to head to Miami, I was talking to a friend of mine who mentioned how fast things seemed to be happening for Coy. He wondered if Coy might get the wrong idea and expect it to always be like that. I reminded him that while things were moving faster than they typically would, Coy had he had gone on approximately 30 auditions since the beginning, booking only 5 jobs. My point was that yeah, things were happening fast, but that doesn't mean that it was easy. He knew what it felt like to be told no.

The week we spent in Florida, much like Vermont, Connecticut, and Los Angeles, was again a wonderful time for our family. They put us up in the Crowne Plaza in Hollywood, Florida which was literally one block from the beach. Coy had a fitting Tuesday evening and then we had a pick up the next morning at 9 to take us to the set. Now this shoot was going to be interesting because for Coy (translation: for us), it was all on location[17]. Meaning, we weren't going to be in the climate controlled comfort of a soundstage. We were going to be outside...in Florida...in May.

The set was exactly like something you would see on television when someone was doing a behind the scenes tour. There were trailers set up all over the place with a few large semi's sprinkled in here and there. People with various jobs were moving around as if whatever they were doing was a matter of

---

[17] *On Location-The location where scenes of a movie or television production are filmed, outside of a studio set.*

life or death. When we arrived, we were greeted by the 2nd 2nd

AD[18]. (no, that's not a typo) She was basically responsible for

Coy and by extension, me. It was her job to make sure Coy was

where he was suppose to be, when he was suppose to be there.

She led us to Coy's trailer and took our breakfast orders. The

inside of the trailer was a small room with a couch, a vanity, a

bathroom, and a television. It wasn't the biggest space but it

was ok. We had moved up a step from just having to stand

around in the heat like we had done when we were extras on

that film in Columbia in the summer of '08.

Coy's wardrobe for the scenes that he was shooting that day

was also in the trailer, along with his sides. He had a few hours

before he had to report to set but he had to go to school, which

was in another trailer in the area. We ate our breakfast and

then were escorted to the classroom. His teacher was a really

nice lady from California who had been doing this kind of work

for a while. There also happened to be another 12 year old boy

---

[18] *2nd 2nd AD-Responsible for the movements of principal actors as well as extras, making sure they are in hair and makeup when needed and prepared to go to set when called.*

in school. He was a regular on the show. He and his mother were really nice and Coy was excited that there was another kid there.

The name of this show is The Glades. It's a cop procedural about a detective from Chicago who has recently relocated to the Miami area and whose method of crime solving frequently rubs the locals the wrong way. Coy's role was that of a young boy (obviously) who discovers a dead body and knows more about it than he's letting on. He was scheduled to shoot five scenes during our week there. It's really interesting because they don't shoot scenes in the order that we see them on television or in the movies. The first scene that Coy shot actually took place during the middle of the show. It was shot outside in front of a beauty salon. As usual, I was a nervous wreck. I don't know why. I think it's because things had happened so fast that every time he started to do something, I wondered if he was truly ready. It's similar to what I was feeling when he started on *A Raisin in the Sun* and *Are We There Yet?*. I was still trying to wrap my brain around the fact that he had done those. Now here he was, sitting on a bike, talking to the director and the star of *The Glades*, going over lines for his scene! Were we really here?! It was just weird.

He did two scenes that day that took place in the same location, but would be shown at different times during the episode. We got back to the room that night at about 8. The next day was actually just a school day. He had no scenes to shoot so they picked us up, took us to the set, Coy did 6 hours of school, and we left. We were done at about 3 and back at the hotel by 3:30. That was a great day because we got to spend the rest of the day at the beach. Keisha and Chayse didn't come to set the first few days. First of all, we were on location and it was hot so Chayse would've been miserable. But more importantly, there was a large pool at the hotel. Coupled with the beach, they had plenty to occupy their time right there.

Coy only had one scene the next day and it just so happened to be the first scene of the day. It was cool to watch because we were on a street in an actual neighborhood. They had blocked the street off so that no cars could come through and they used people from the neighborhood as background. Coy's scene took place in someone's driveway, again with Matt Passmore, the lead actor. The scene wasprobably a total of 45 seconds on screen but it took about two and a half hours to shoot. Afterwards, he did his necessary hours of school, and we were done for the day. We got back to the hotel at about 5 and hung out at the pool for the rest of the day. One of the great things about all of this is the fact that we get to spend so much time together. Its hard work but we also have a lot of fun.

Coy's next two scenes took place at a location in another city. Homestead, Fl was about an hour from where we were. They took us down one evening and checked us in to yet another hotel. The next morning, Coy and I were driven about twenty miles to the set location which was in the middle of a sugarcane field. When we got there, the scene was much like it was on the first day we arrived. There were trailers and a few 18 wheelers spread out in various positions. Coy's tutor was already there in the trailer that was designated for school. We were escorted to

Coy's trailer where he changed into his wardrobe and we ate breakfast.

In this scene, Coy's character and a few friends are chasing rabbits through the sugarcane field, when he stumbles upon the dead body. Now, for those of you who have never been in a sugarcane field, imagine stems of asparagus that are about 2 inches in circumference and over six feet tall. So he and the other boys had to actually run through the sugarcane as if they were chasing rabbits, in 90 degree weather. They had plenty of water and there was a canopy where the boys would be between shots. But it was still very hot and sticky and it was difficult running through the sugarcane. I knew that this would be tough for Coy but I also knew that he could do it. I thought it was a great opportunity for him. He was in a position that called for him to push himself beyond what he thought he could do. After several takes, he was hot, tired, irritated, and had some minor scratches from running through the sugarcane. A couple of times, I pulled him to the side and said that he could stop if he wanted to. I could easily tell them that these were very difficult circumstances and I didn't want him doing it. But he didn't want to. He said that it was hard but he was still having fun and he wanted to finish what he started. And he did. He finished the difficult shoot that day and also did another morning of shooting in the same location. There was no running during the morning shoot but it was *extremely* hot. Once he finished his last scene, we had lunch with the rest of the cast and crew in the meal tent. When we were leaving, the 2nd AD called an episode wrap [19]for him and everyone gave him a big applause. It was really nice.

Production had sent a driver to pick Keisha and Chayse up from the hotel and bring them to the set. That way, we could leave from there and head straight back to the Crowne Plaza. We were scheduled to fly back to Columbia the next morning. As we headed back to the hotel, I told him that I was very proud of him. I told him that I knew that it hadn't been easy but instead of quitting, he pushed himself further than he probably thought

---

[19] *Episode Wrap-When a regular cast member or guest star has finished all of his or her scenes in a television episode.*

he could. I said that every time he sees that episode, he would be reminded of how strong he is.

One of the cool things about shooting the episode was getting a chance to work with the tutor, Wendy Herron. Unlike the tutor on the set of *Are We There Yet,* Wendy did more than just teach school. The state of California requires production companies operating under its laws to provide a state licensed studio teacher/social worker if there are minors in their production. Their job is to ensure that the production company is following the law when it comes to their treatment of minors. They have to make sure that the kids are getting the required breaks, not working longer than they are suppose to, and are safe at all times. Keisha and I feel like this is our responsibility as parents but it was nice to have someone else there who had our child's best interest at heart. And boy was she great! She was really knowledgeable about the laws and didn't hesitate to let them know when it was time for a break or how much longer they had before they had to release him. She really was amazing. We all hope we get to work with her again someday.

23

THE DISNEY TRIP

We got back to Columbia on Wednesday and were set to fly to
Orlando on Friday to do the *Are We There Yet* radio press
junket. We relaxed for a couple of days and then it was back on
the road again. A car service picked us up at about 6am on
Friday and we headed for the airport. We arrived in Orlando
and had a driver waiting for us. They had us staying at the Beach
Club Resort and when we got there, our room wasn't ready yet.
The concierge took our luggage and held it for us while we went
and got something to eat and explored the resort a little bit. It
was really nice. We had been to Disney World several times
since Coy was about 4 and had stayed at one of the smaller
resorts once. We usually stayed at a hotel off of the Disney
property because it was cheaper. But this... was nice!

After an hour or so, they told us that the room was ready and that we could head up and they would bring us our luggage. We got upstairs, unlocked the door, and headed into the room. It was a nice room with two queen beds to the left, a 46 inch flat screen on a dresser to the right, a bathroom, and a small balcony. Coy walked in first.

"It's smaller than I thought it was going to be but it's nice." he said.

But as he continued to walk into the room, there was another door right past the dresser. I couldn't see what was through the door, but I could see the look on his face. It was one of pure joy and then he disappeared through the door. When I got to the door myself, it was like the gates of heaven (or at the very least, the gates of the Magic Kingdom) had been opened.

We were in the Presidential Suite which consisted of the room that we initially came in, a dining room next to it, a large living room, a sun room, another bedroom with a king bed and bathroom, and three entrances into the suite, with another bathroom next to the main entrance. Whew! The room was amazing. And this is coming from someone who has traveled a lot in my lifetime. I've stayed in hotels all over the world. Trust me, this was nice! As we walked around looking at everything, we realized that we were so excited when we entered the room, we had missed the gift package that TBS had left for Coy. It was a small cooler with the AWTY logo on it. Inside, there were various items that had pictures of the cast along with the AWTY logo... such as "Kevin's cookies", etc. There was also a brand new Nintendo DS, which of course Coy thought was really cool. The sun room was beautiful. It was shaped in a circle with hardwood floors and the windows gave us a view of the Beach.

The only problem with the room, which we all quickly realized, was that we wouldn't be there long enough to really enjoy it. It was already Friday afternoon. Coy had the radio junket on Saturday morning and then we would be at the parks for the rest of the day, then on Sunday morning, we were leaving. We got over that quickly though and decided not to dwell on the negative. We would have a good time and just enjoy it while we were there.

Another perk that we got was a full time guide while we were there. He worked for Disney and was assigned to us for the entire weekend. His job was to basically make sure we had everything we needed, and take us anywhere we needed to go. He was also our guide for the parks, which I didn't fully understand until we actually got to the parks. He was a really nice guy and we were glad that he had been assigned to us. He called the room and said that he was downstairs and ready to go whenever we were. Coy didn't have anything to do until the next morning so we figured we'd hit the parks. We piled into the SUV that was designated to us and Kevin took us to the Magic Kingdom. Now this is where my earlier statement about not fully understanding what it meant to have Kevin as our guide for the parks, comes into play. We didn't go to the main entrance. He drove through an employee access gate and we parked in the "behind the scenes" area. He escorted us through a small maze and we ended up entering through a door that put us like right in the middle of the park. Then whenever we got to a ride that we wanted to get on, he would lead us through some

side entrance and we would end up at the front of the line,

where we would be put on the ride immediately. It was

unbelievable. Kevin had on a vest that was a different color that

the one's being worn by the people working the rides. I

assumed that this meant that he had VIP clients because as

soon as they saw him, they would simply ask "how many" and

then proceed to get us on the ride. The people waiting in line

who we had skipped however, had no idea who we were. We

had *AWTY* badges around our necks but seeing as how the show

had yet to be aired, this meant nothing to them. We were

simply the people who were cutting in front of them. No one

said anything to us directly but there were some looks ranging

from "I wonder who they are?" to "Who the hell do they think

they are?"

Having been to Disney World several times and lived the

experience of standing in line for 45 minutes waiting to get on a

ride that would last a minute and thirty seconds, I could totally

understand how some of the people must have been feeling. At the same time, it is that experience that allowed me to enjoy the perks of what we were involved in. We had stood in the lines and now we were fortunate enough to not have to. With the exception of Chayse. He was only 3 at the time and had never been to Disney World. I told Keisha that this was a terrible precedent to set because the next time we came, it would probably be on our own dime and we would be right back in the lines with everyone else. Chayse of course would be confused as to why we don't just go to the front like last time!

After about an hour of riding, we left and went to Epcot and did the same thing. We would ride some of the rides two or three times in a row. We left Epcot and went back to Magic Kingdom and hooked up with Essence and Jaime and Jaime's niece for dinner. After that, it was time to head back to the hotel. Coy had an early call time the next day.

The radio junket was interesting. The best way to describe it is that it is like speed dating for radio interviews. TBS had invited approximately 25-30 on air radio personalities from cities all over the country. The plan was to have the cast do 5- 10 minute interviews with each of them that they would then take back to their station and play sparingly, leading up to the premiere of the show. Coy and I got downstairs at about 7:30 that morning. There were three conference rooms designated for the junket. One was for breakfast for us, the second was used as the interview room, and the third was for the DJ's and their family to hang out. In this room there were two big screens set up that had a couple of episodes of the show playing. They also had a couple of televisions with Wii game consoles hooked up for the kids. It was a nice set up.

The junket started at 8 and was pretty simple. Coy and Teala did their interviews together, Terry and Essence did theirs together, and Ice Cube did his alone. There were six booths set up with a DJ at each booth and the cast would do a 5- 10 minute interview, then move on to the next booth until they had done all 6. There would be a five minute break while the next set of DJ's came in, and then they would start the process again. This went on until they all had done an interview with every DJ. It was a great way to get in a lot of press for the show in a short period of time. I thought it was great for Coy as well. At that point, I don't think he had ever done an interview. But much like filming three episodes of the show in a week, this interview "boot camp" was a great way for him to learn how to do it.

Keisha and Chayse came down about an hour into it and had breakfast. After that, Kevin took them to the outlets to hang out until Coy was done. The junket lasted until about noon and then we were free until that night. We spent the rest of the day at the parks and had a blast! That night, there was a dinner planned for all of us. It was a really nice set up at some sort of VIP room at Magic Kingdom .They invited the cast and all of their family members plus all of the radio DJ's and their families as well. We got a chance to mingle with everyone and the DJ's and their families took pictures with the cast. After dinner, we were all escorted to a location in the park where they served dessert while we watched a fireworks display. It was a really good night .The next morning we were up bright and early, heading to the airport to catch our flight back to Columbia. It had been our best trip to Disney by far!!

24

THE PREMIERE

Back when we were in LA, we made plans to watch the premiere of *Are We There Yet?* with Mike and Trina. They planned a vacation in Myrtle Beach, SC for that week so that our families could be together. Upon our return from Orlando, we had a week to kill before we headed to the beach. We stayed with Keisha's sister at her Dad's house during that time and just relaxed. Although it was kind of nice to not have anything to do for a while, the week went by kind of slow because we were really looking forward to going to the beach and hanging out with everyone.

During our week in Columbia, Coy had a couple of interviews with local press. The first was a news show on the Columbia CBS affiliate, WLTX. *Friends @Five* is a newscast hosted by evening anchors Darci Strickland and Andrea Mock. They were kind enough to have Coy on to talk about the show and his experiences in the industry. A couple of days later we took him to one of the radio stations, 103.9, where he did an interview with one of the on-air DJ's, "Neek". After having traveled all over, it was nice to be able to come home and get some love from our hometown.

The following Tuesday, we met the Curry's at a gas station near where we were staying and followed them down to Myrtle Beach. There were 14 of us total in an 8 bedroom house right on the beach. Once we got settled, we took the boys to the beach along with Crysten, Mike, (2 of Mike and Trina's 4 kids), and one of Crysten's friends that had come along. It was nice to be with people that we knew so well. Being there was just like being on any other vacation that we had taken together over the years. We appreciated this because things had gotten a little crazy in Columbia.

It's amazing how what Coy was doing and what our family was going through had changed some people's perception of us. All of a sudden, we were getting phone calls from people we hadn't heard from in years. "Let's get together." "You need to bring the boys by for a visit." "When are you guys coming over for dinner?" Really?? It was crazy because since we settled in Columbia after I retired, we barely heard from most of these people. We have always had a very small circle of friends in Columbia. Which was ok with us. I mean, I'd rather have to two true friends than 20 so-called friends. So we were ok with that. But all of a sudden, everyone wanted in. Which was crazy to me because our life was nothing like what most of them probably thought it was like. We heard rumors about how much money Coy was making (he was already a millionaire!), which was ridiculous because we had never disclosed that to ANYONE, so it was all speculation. Anyway, it was nice to kind of hide away for awhile.

So, we finally made it to Wednesday night. Premiere night. They were airing two episodes back to back. All 14 of us gathered in the living room and prepared to watch the show. Seeing it on television, with commercial breaks and everything, was an experience that I can't describe in words. Our son was on national television. I know I have used this word a lot so far...but it was *crazy*! Seriously. Everyone at the house was excited and said that they loved the show. We got several calls from people saying how much they liked the show and how well Coy did. It was a great night.

Later that night as I was falling asleep, I thought about everything that had happened up to that point. I thought about the comments that had been made about Coy along the way. In addition to what the agents in LA and the people involved with *Raisin* had said, the people he had worked with since then were also very impressed with him. When he did the *CarQuest* commercial in North Carolina, the director said that Coy was a joy to work with and was a gifted actor. When he did the ten episodes of *Are We There Yet?*, people were amazed that he had just recently started. They said that he was so natural and so good, that it was like he had been doing this his whole life.

The director from *The Glades* and co-stars Matt Passmore and Michelle Hurd were also impressed with him. The director said that Coy was very talented and he looked forward to working with him again. It was great hearing all of these comments but up until that point, that's all they were...comments. Seeing him on television made it real.

We spent the rest of the time at Myrtle Beach, getting up and hitting the beach first thing in the morning every day, hitting the outlets, and just enjoying each others company. Before we left, Mike told me that he was putting on a basketball camp the following week in Putnam County, Ga, which is near their home. He said that if we didn't have anything going on, we should come stay with them for that week and let Coy go to the basketball camp. Keisha and I talked to Coy about it and he was excited. He said that he would love to go. That was the great thing about him through all of this. He never got caught up in the whole Hollywood/being on tv thing. He just wanted to be a kid.

On Thursday, a week after the show premiered, we headed back to Columbia. We were there for the weekend. We unpacked (again), washed clothes (again), and then packed (again). On Sunday evening, we headed to Reynolds, Ga which is where the Curry's were living. We were all looking forward to it because it was going to be like another little vacation. Reynolds is a secluded town off of I20, between Augusta and Atlanta. They lived in a gated community that was surrounded by woods and a beautiful golf course. They had a huge house so there was plenty of room for all of us to be very, very comfortable.

We got up Monday at 7, ate breakfast, and headed to Putnam County for the camp. It was about a 20 minute drive from where we were. There was actually a total of about eight of us in two car loads. Mike had two of his friends that had come down to help with the camp, one of them had his son, and then there were two more boys staying at the house as well. Their parents were friends of Mike and Trina and they had come down for the week to attend the camp. We were all staying at the house so the atmosphere was...festive to say the least. I had also decided to help out with the camp. First of all, it was something that I had been doing for years when I played and through my training company before Coy started acting. It had been a while so I was looking forward to it. Second, I wanted to run the group that Coy was going to be in. The show had just premiered the week before and it was going to be on during the week of camp. I didn't know if the kids had seen it or if they were going to watch it that week and I didn't know how they would react to Coy but in any case, I wanted to be there with him. It was more for my piece of mind than anything else.

Coy has been playing basketball since he was 5. I coached him until he was about 8 and then I started coaching girls high school basketball. He was always by my side during those days. During practices, he would have the little brothers of my players on the sidelines, running them through the same drills that I ran my players through. During games, he would be on the bench. Getting towels and water for the players and cheering them on. Basketball is in his blood so he was really looking forward to this camp.

I really enjoyed watching him have fun with the other kids. I thought about all of the things we had been through in the last year, the places we had been, the auditions Coy had gone on, stuff he had filmed. As much fun as it was for him, he hadn't really had the chance to just be a kid. To be around other kids his age and just do what kids do. Time seemed to stand still while he was at camp and he was just having a blast. It was the best thing that we could have done for him at that time.

During that first day of camp, Keisha got a call from Ericka DeAbreu. The casting agency in Charlotte that Coy had booked the CarQuest commercial through, had requested him to audition for a national commercial that they were casting for. Keisha told us when we got back to the house that day and Coy was not happy. Going would mean that he would miss one day of the basketball camp and he was not trying to hear that. He hit us with, "But you said that I didn't have to do anything that I didn't want to do." This was a tough decision for us because on the one hand, he was right, we did say that. But at the same time, this career was something that he had chosen to do. We explained to him that at this point, we were still in the process of building his career so if he wanted to have the opportunity to do more television and possibly even films, he had to take pretty much any opportunity that came his way. He wasn't happy, but he eventually agreed to do it.

We left Tuesday after camp and headed back to Columbia. The audition was at 2 in the afternoon on Wednesday in Charlotte which is a drive that we could have made in about three and a half hours from Reynolds, but I thought that it would be better to just stay in Columbia on Tuesday night, let Coy get a good night's sleep and then take the hour drive to Charlotte Wednesday. It would be kind of difficult to have to audition for something after being in a car for three hours. We got back to Columbia at about 7 Tuesday evening and just relaxed for the rest of the night.

The next day, we headed to Charlotte at about 12:30. Auditions at this casting agency were always crazy to me because it was a two hour trip there and back but we would only be in their office for 10 minutes. Such is the life of an actor! Sometimes, you gotta do what you gotta do! We got there about 15 minutes early, Coy went in and did his thing, and we headed back to Reynolds. We stopped and got something to eat, stopped again so that Chayse could use the restroom, and stopped again so Coy could use the restroom. All in all, what should have been about a three hour trip turned into a four and a half hour trip. We got back to Reynolds and settled in to get ready to watch the second week of the show.

Seeing Coy on television during the second week, had pretty much the same effect on me as it had the previous week. I still hadn't gotten use to it and a part of me hopes that I never do. Don't get me wrong. I don't think for one second that Coy is better than any other kid because he's on television. Nor do I think that my wife and I are any better than any other parents because our child is on a sitcom. While I have always been a fan of film and television, I've never been one to put celebrities on a pedestal just because they happen to be on television. To me, they have always just been people. Like anyone else. It just so happens that what they do for a living, puts them in a situation where they are recognized by people that they don't know. I think my experience as a basketball player is what gives me that perspective. I can remember a few times when I was in college or playing in Europe when I would be approached by someone who would want an autograph or a picture, or wanted to pay for my meal in a restaurant. I never understood why. I would always think to myself, "Why? I'm just a guy. I'm no different than you."

So seeing Coy on television didn't have that kind of effect on me. I was just so overwhelmed with pride. Just two years prior to this, he wasn't afraid to say what he wanted to do. He didn't care if people told him that he was crazy, that a kid from Columbia, SC could never do something like that. He just stated what he wanted to do and set out to do it. And while there is a lot of luck involved, I believe that your attitude goes a long way in determining what you accomplish. Watching him on television meant more to me than simple words can describe. It meant that he listened to his Mother and me for all those years. Preaching to him that you can do anything you want if you believe in yourself and are willing to put the work in. It meant that he believed that he was capable of anything. It meant that all of the auditions and callbacks he had gone on without getting the job, never discouraged him. He never doubted himself and his belief never faltered. He inspired me more than I've ever been because he showed me that dreams really do come true.

The show was good that night and Coy was great. The next day, like I had done the previous week, I scoured the internet, looking for ratings information. As I mentioned earlier, TBS had a pick-up option on the show for 90 episodes. I had no idea what the criteria was for getting the pick up. What I did know was that a few years prior, TBS had the same option for *House of Payne*, a Tyler Perry show that was enjoying continued success on the network. It was difficult to compare though because that show had a different 10 episode pilot process. They aired only in select cities before TBS picked it up for national broadcast. So their initial ratings requirements may have been different from ours anyway.

House of Payne was now considered a hit for TBS so I thought that comparing our ratings to theirs would give me some kind of barometer to determine how we were doing. The premiere night ratings for the first two episodes (3.2 million for the first, 3.3 million for the second) were solid. Not spectacular, but good. I knew that the numbers would drop a little during the second week, which they did (2.6 mil for the first ep, 2.7 for the second), but I felt like as long as we stayed in the range that House of Payne was in, we would be ok. I mean, they did get the 90 episode pick up that we were looking for. The night of the second week of our show, House of Payne did 1.7 mil and 2.4 mil, so I felt good about where we were.

Camp was interesting the next day. The other kids hadn't seen Coy in person since the end of the day on Tuesday. He wasn't at camp on Wednesday, and on Wednesday night, they saw him on television. When we arrived on Thursday, many of them thought that Coy left to go do the show that they had just seen him on the night before. (Seriously) Some of them asked where his sister was and why she wasn't at the basketball camp. Some wanted to know how it felt to have a dad that was famous (Terry Crews, not me.) It was funny. I took a few minutes and explained to them how it all worked. I let Coy answer a few questions and then we got the day started. Some of them were a little star struck with Coy for a little while but by lunch, things were back to normal.

On Friday at the end of the week, we present awards to the kids for different things that they participate in during the week. There are 5 on 5, 3 on 3, 1 on 1, lay up, and free throw competitions that all of the winners receive trophies for. We also present trophies for the Most Valuable Player and the Michael Curry Award which is for the child that has the best attitude all week. I ran this group along with another counselor and we had to consult on the Most Valuable Player and Michael Curry awards. I felt like Coy deserved the Michael Curry Award. He is just that kind of kid. He is a decently skilled player who loves to win but other people's feelings are more important. He is always encouraging other kids and never has a bad attitude. But because he is my son and I was over the group, I didn't feel comfortable suggesting that he receive one of the awards. To my delight, when we started discussing the possible candidates for the two awards, my co-counselor mentioned Coy first. He said that he felt it was a no-brainer in his opinion that Coy deserved the Michael Curry Award.

We started the presentation and began giving out the awards. Coy's 5 on 5 team had won that competition so he received an award for that. The Most Valuable Player and Michael Curry awards were given out last. The MVP went first to a kid who was clearly the most talented player in the group. When I began to speak about the Michael Curry award, I quickly glanced at Coy. He was looking in another direction, not really paying full attention to me. When I called his name out, one of the kids had to tap him on his shoulder to tell him that I had just called his name. He looked at me and then pointed at himself. "Me??" I said, "Yeah! Come on up here." He was so excited. It was great to see him so happy. I was proud of him yet again.

25

WEST COAST BOUND

On Saturday, we headed back to Columbia. During camp week,

Keisha had been speaking to Coy's publicist, Shannon Barr, who

thought that it would be a good idea for us to get some updated

photos of Coy. Now that the show was on, she wanted to start

scheduling some print and radio interviews. The print interviews

would require her to submit a photo. At that point, Coy hadn't

taken pictures in about a year. That may not seem like a lot of

time but an 11 year old kid can change quite a bit in a year.

There was a particular photographer that she used for her

clients that was supposed to be really good. His rates were

reasonable but there was one catch...we would have to take

Coy out to LA.

As things were still financially tight for us at the time, this was a tough decision for us. When we decided to take this journey, we said that we were going to do it together. This meant having to buy three tickets to LA, hotel, rental car, food, gas, plus the photographers fee. After some consideration, we decided that it was something that we needed to do to further Coy's career. We had Shannon set the photo shoot for the following Saturday. While I was in the process of making our travel arrangements, Jaime and Essence came to mind. I thought that it would be great to see them while we were out there so I called to let them know that we were coming.They asked me where we were staying and I said that I wasn't sure yet. Then, they did something unexpected...they invited us to stay with them. I was really surprised but respectfully declined. I told them that we appreciated the gesture but didn't want to intrude on them. Their response was that they understood but since we were only going to be there for a couple of days, there was no reason for us to spend money on a hotel when they had all that room at their house. It was an amazing and unselfish offer and I could tell that they genuinely meant it. We graciously accepted their offer and I crossed that off of my to do list.

We traveled to LA on Thursday so that Coy would have all of Friday to just relax and rest. We wanted to make sure that he had plenty of energy and was himself for the photo shoot. On Friday, we went to a mall in Sherman Oaks so that Keisha could find a couple of more outfits for him for the shoot. We kind of just hung out at Essence and Jaime's the rest of the day. They have a pool in the backyard which the boys LOVE so we went swimming for a while and just relaxed the rest of the day.

On Saturday morning, we took Coy to get a haircut, went back to the house so that he could shower and change, then headed to the studio where the shoot was to take place. It just so happened to be in the same neighborhood, about 5 minutes from where we were staying. We arrived and the photographer greeted us at the gate and led us to the back of the property where the studio was located. His assistant was there getting everything set up. Jamie also came which was nice. It was great to have her input because she knows what the industry wants in terms of looks. Keisha, Jamie, Keith, and his assistant went through all of the clothes that we had brought for Coy and decided on a few outfits.

When the shoot began, I was really impressed with what Coy was doing. It was his third such photo shoot and the first one I had seen since he started at DeAbreu two years before. He was posing and smiling and laughing like this was something he did all the time. He had his IPod with him and they let him play whatever music he wanted. The energy was great! They did a few different outfits inside the studio and then took some shots outside. It took about two hours total. Coy had a great time and we ended up getting the shots we needed.

We headed back to the Mendez's and started packing our stuff. We were on the red eye that night, scheduled to leave at midnight. At about 9pm, we packed our stuff into the rental car, thanked our gracious hosts, and headed to LAX. Once there, we learned that our flight was overbooked. When we got to the gate, they were trying to get people to give up their seats for travel vouchers. When I made our roundtrip flight arrangements, I only purchased three seats. Chayse was still three years old so we always flew with him as a lap child. When it was time to board the plane, I was told that I needed to purchase a ticket for Chayse. I explained to them that our tickets were roundtrip, which meant that we had flown to LA, on their airline, with Chayse as a lap child. Why was it different now? Their explanation was that whoever allowed us to board the flight without a seat for him had simply made a mistake. FAA regulations required a child his age to have their own seat.

I went back and forth with them for a few minutes and finally relented. "Ok, let me just buy a ticket then." "I'm sorry sir, we have no more seats available." Really?? Anyway, it all ended up working out in our favor. Because they were already offering travel vouchers for people willing to give up their seats, we were able to get three vouchers and use one of them right away to purchase a ticket for Chayse. The problem was, they wouldn't have any flights available until Tuesday at midnight. But, as it turns out, this wasn't going to be a problem after all. Two days prior to all of this, Jamie told us that she had secured two tickets to the premiere of the Disney Channel original movie, *16 Wishes*. While it wasn't a big time Hollywood movie premiere, it was still a big deal for Coy. It would be his first premiere and a chance for him to walk the red carpet amongst other child actors which was a great way to generate press. At the time, we were scheduled to leave on Saturday night which meant that he wasn't going to be able to go to the premiere which was on Tuesday night. But the developments at the airport had changed all of that. Since we were on the red eye on Tuesday night, he would be able to attend, at least for a little while.

Because we had given up our seats, the airline gave us a voucher for a hotel room for the night. They retrieved our luggage off of the plane and we took the shuttle over to the Crowne Plaza near the airport. By the time we got into the room, it was almost 2am and needless to say, we were all exhausted! Everyone was also starving but at that time of the night without a car, there was no way to get anything. So we raided the vending machine and called it a night.

The next day (Sunday) was Fathers day as well as my birthday. We got up, took showers, got dressed, and began to formulate a plan. The first thing we had to do was get some food! There was a Denny's about 3/4 mile from the hotel so we walked there for breakfast. We decided to check out of the hotel, get another rental car, and check into another hotel in LA. That would be more fun than staying out near the airport for two days. The rental car place was about a mile from where the Denny's was. It was a beautiful day so we decided to walk. We got the car and returned to the hotel to collect our things and check out. As we were driving away from the hotel, I told Keisha to call Ess and Jaime to let them know that we were still in town. They would be expecting to hear from us once we got home safely and I didn't want them to worry. When they realized that we were still there, Jaime said, "So you guys are

coming over, right?"

"Yeah." I replied. "We'll come hang out. Once we check into a hotel and put our stuff in our room, we'll be over."

"Check into a hotel?" he asked. "Why would you do that? Why not just stay with us?"

"Listen." I told him. "You guys were already gracious enough to let us stay with you for three days and we REALLY appreciate it. We do not want to wear out our welcome. It's fine, really. It'll just be two days."

Essence got on the phone...

"You guys better get back over here right now." She said. "You

will be staying with us until you leave.

End of discussion."...and handed the phone back to Jaime.

"I guess you heard that, right?" he said.

"We're on our way." I replied. So we headed back to the

Mendez's.

It was a beautiful day in LA that day, so when we got back to the

house, they were relaxing at the pool. We put our suitcases in

our room, changed, and the boys and I jumped in. We played in

the pool for awhile and then all went and got some dinner at

the Cheesecake Factory. On Monday, Jaime and Essence

decided to have a Bar B Que. They invited some friends over

and we had a nice dinner outside by the pool. On Tuesday, we

went to a couple of stores to find Coy something to wear to the

premiere. That night was going to be his first red carpet and he wanted to look good!

Our schedule for Tuesday night was a little hectic. Our flight was scheduled to leave at 11:30 that night, which meant that we needed to be at the airport no later than 10. We had to turn in the rental car first so that meant that we had to head out that way at about 9. The premiere was at the Harmony Gold Theater in LA, about 20 minutes from where Jaime and Essence lived. The red carpet started at 7 but the actual movie didn't start until 8. Coy's manager was only able to get two tickets so the plan was that Coy and I would go, (again, I insisted that Keisha go with him but she declined) he would do the red carpet, we would watch the first 30 minutes of the movie, then leave, pick Keisha and Chayse up, and head out to the airport by 9. Whew!

Although I had seen coverage of premieres and watched people walk down the red carpet on television, I really had no idea what it was going to be like. Coy and I showed up in our rented

Ford Flex and had it valet parked right next to the BMW's, Mercedes', and other luxury cars that had chauffeured some of Hollywood's most famous "tweens" to the event. We arrived a little early and were greeted by one of the assistants to his publicist. We saw Shannon soon after that. She had other, more known clients attending the premiere but she never made Coy feel like he was less important than any of them. I've always appreciated that. It may sound like it's not that big of a deal...treating people as equals. But in that world where it's all about *who* you are, it's a very big deal.

While we waited for them to start the red carpet, we hit the gifting booths! The gifting booths are set up at these premieres for different companies to promote their products. They basically give their products to celebrities in exchange for a picture of them holding it. (or wearing it, or sitting on it, or drinking it...you get the picture) There were some nice items that Coy got from some of the booths but the biggest was a brand new Ripstick. Although he already had one at home, he thought that it was really cool that he got a new one for free.

Soon after, it was time for him to hit the red carpet. Shannon came and got him and escorted him to the carpet. It was soooo crowded in that area that I decided to stay back so I didn't actually see him walk the carpet. When he was done, it was time to head into the theater. It was almost 8:00 and we had to leave at 8:30. This was kind of exciting for me because I've always wondered what actually happened at movie premieres. This wasn't the premiere of a summer blockbuster, but it was a premiere nonetheless. Once everyone got into the theater and was seated, the star and producers of the movie got on stage and spoke. I thought it was really cool because we got to hear from the people who were involved with making the movie. I assume that this happens at the premiere of every film.

When they were done, I was wondering, what happens if the

movie sucks? How awkward is that? For everyone. A lot of the people in the audience at the premiere of a film are friends and family of those involved with making the film. What do they do if they don't like it?? Just a thought. Anyway...By the time they were done talking and the film started, it was 8:15. Coy and I stayed until 8:30 and then snuck out. It would have been nice to stay for the entire movie and then attend the after party but we had to go. We headed back to the house to get Keisha and Chayse, said our goodbyes, and headed to LAX. We were finally on our way back to the east coast. What started out as a quick three day trip turned into a six day trip with a movie premiere thrown in. Not bad. We had a really good time and especially enjoyed being able to see Jaime and Essence again.

26

HIDING OUT

We got back to Charlotte early Wednesday morning and drove

back to Columbia to Keisha's sister's house. After the all night

flight, we were exhausted so we pretty much slept the whole

day. Before we left to head out to LA, Trina and Mike had

invited us back to Reynold's when we returned. They said that

we were welcomed to come and stay as long as we'd like if we

wanted to just get away. It was so peaceful there that we didn't

hesitate to take them up on their offer. We were scheduled to

head to Philadelphia for the *Electric Company* at the beginning

of July so we figured we'd just relax there until it was time to

go. Our time spent on set in Stamford back in January and

February taught us that there were long days ahead of us.

We spent the night in Columbia and caught the show at Keisha's sister's house. The next afternoon, we loaded up the truck and headed back to Reynolds, Ga. Coy had a phone interview with Goom Radio that Shannon had set up the week before. Goom Radio is an internet radio company that has various internet radio stations that cater to different genres. Zang Radio is the pop genre station for the company that's geared towards teens. He spoke with Zach Sang and The Student Body, an energetic bunch that made it fun and interesting for Coy. They called while we were on the road. That day also happened to be Coy's 12th birthday. Keisha and I had ordered a new cell phone that he wanted. It was waiting for him at his Godparent's house. Once we got there, they had a gift waiting for him as well. They had bought him a new Macbook. So he had a pretty good birthday.

For the next week or so, we...did...nothing. Literally. We slept in everyday, watched movies, I read a lot. But it was really just a relaxing time that we didn't even realize we needed until we were in the midst of it. This was the last week of June, 2010.

Since June of 2009, we had been traveling. From South Carolina to New York (several times), Vermont, Connecticut, Los Angeles, Orlando, Miami. We had moved out of our house, and stayed in more hotels than I can count. And when we *weren't* traveling, we were thinking about and planning the next time we *would* have to travel. Not only had the last year been physically exhausting, but it was also mentally and emotionally draining as well. As much as we all loved what Coy was doing and as exciting as it was, there were times that we wished we were just at home doing what we normally do. Coy outside playing with his friends. Keisha messing around in the kitchen. Me in the driveway washing the cars while Chayse drove his car around. Just the normal, non-glamorous life that we had before all of this started. But we all knew that there were going to be some sacrifices on this journey. Being together is what made it easier.

The next week on Thursday or Friday, we went to the movies to see the Karate Kid remake with Jaden Smith. We have always been huge fans of the Smith family and had wanted to see the movie, but hadn't had a chance. As I watched it, I couldn't help but compare Coy and Jaden. I mean they're the same age and have similar features. I wasn't comparing them to see who was better. I happen to think that Jaden is super talented. I was trying to see how Coy measured up. He had been on stage and television, but he hadn't been on the big screen yet. I was trying to see if I could "see" him up there.

I thought that the movie was great. I felt like Jaden proved that he could carry a movie. But I also left feeling like, "Coy could do that." Not meaning that he could do a better job than Jaden, just...he could do that. I could see him on the big screen holding his own. At the end of the movie when the credits were rolling, they were showing various production pictures of Will and Jada (who were producers) with Jaden. Seeing those pictures really inspired me. *That's* what I want to do. They had taken control of

their professional lives and the result was that they now had the

power to help *their* kids realize their dreams. Will and Jada

entered the business separately and reached a level of success

separate of each other. Now, they're doing it together. I love it!

I really felt like we could do the same thing. I may not be an

actor, but Coy is. I love to write. I didn't see any reason why we

couldn't create something like that for our family. Seeing that

movie made me feel like we were on the right path. I was really

inspired and excited about what the future could hold.

27

AN ELECTRIC SUMMER

A couple of days later, I got a call from John Shea. The contract

for The Electric Company had been completed so it was time to

sign, and get ready to head to New York. Wait...New York?? Yep.

NYC. Apparently, the production location had been changed

from Philadelphia to New York at the last minute. They wanted

Coy in the city on Monday, July 5th. He had a table read on

Tuesday and the first day of shooting was on Wednesday. We

signed all of the paperwork and faxed it back to John. The next

day, Friday, we headed back to Columbia to prepare for our

flight on Monday.

Coy was scheduled to shoot 12 episodes of the show from July 7

through September 7. They would put us up in a one bedroom

apartment and provide weekly per diem for Coy and one parent

for the duration. This was in addition to the per episode salary

he would receive. It was very much like when I played

basketball in Europe. This time, we washed and packed while in

Reynolds. We had a couple of outfits for the weekend but when

we headed back to Columbia, we were basically ready to go.

TBS and PBS, while they sound the same, are really quite

different. Working for one is nothing like working for the other.

But this is not a dig at PBS. The people we ended up working

with on *The Electric Company* were amazing. They simply don't

have the financial resources available to them that a cable

network like TBS does. However, they make the most out of

what they do have. On Sunday when we got ready to leave,

there was no car service provided by PBS to take us to the

airport. Keisha's sister took us in her Toyota Camry. There was a

car waiting for us at LaGuardia in New York but instead of a

brand new spacious Cadillac Escalade, we squeezed into an old

Lincoln Towncar with all of our luggage. Our destination wasn't

the Four Seasons or the Presidential Suite at the Beach Club

Resort. We were taken to the Ameritania Hotel in the Theater

District. But none of it mattered to us. We were excited to be

there and thankful for the opportunity. As for the hotel, I'm

sure that the person from *The Electric Company* who made this

reservation thought it was a nice place. I mean, I looked it up on

the internet before we left and the pictures looked great. But,

as is often the case, perception is not always reality.

The lobby was nice. But once we got upstairs, it was like we

were in an Alfred Hitchcock movie. The hallway was small, dark,

and grungy. The room was worse than that. It looked like it

hadn't been cleaned in months. There was dust everywhere, the

carpet was filthy, and the bathroom was so small that I couldn't

sit on the toilet because my knees were banging the door! At

this point, it was already after 9 pm. We were tired and hungry

and had an early day the next morning. We thought about going to another hotel for the night but decided to just stick it out.

Our apartment wouldn't be ready until Thursday so we would

call TEC first thing the next morning and request another hotel

until then.

We were only a few blocks from Times Square so we decided to

walk down and get something to eat. It was about 9:30 now and

it was hooooot!! It was like we were in an oven! Leaving South

Carolina in July, we were looking forward to a New York

summer but it was like the heat had packed a bag and gotten on

the plane with us in Columbia. We figured that it was just a hot

night. Little did we know that it was a sign of things to come.

Times Square was buzzing with energy, as usual. But we were

tired and just looking for something to eat. We settled on Bubba

Gumps. After dinner, we headed back to the hotel.

The next morning, Coy had to be at the Sesame Workshop

offices for a table read. I got up early and walked down to

McDonald's to get breakfast for everyone. By the time I got back, Keisha was on the phone with someone at Sesame explaining our concerns about the hotel. They were very apologetic and started looking for another hotel immediately. Before we left to head to the offices, they called us back to let us know that they had made a reservation for us at a Holiday Inn two blocks away. The problem was the room wouldn't be ready until after 2. We didn't have time to take our stuff over before we left so we just packed it up and I figured I could come back and get it and take it over to the Holiday Inn after lunch.

The table read was at the Sesame office, the same place that Coy and I had gone to back in March when he auditioned. We took a taxi and arrived about 15 min early. This gave us time to meet everyone in the office. Coy and I had already met a few of them. We immediately got a feeling of family amongst everyone there. They were all really nice and it seemed like a really warm, inviting atmosphere.

The table read started right at 10. Keisha, Chayse, and I sat in the waiting room watching television. After an hour or so, I headed back to our hotel. It turns out that we were only about 15 blocks away. The weather was nice, so I decided to walk. I got back to the hotel and collected all of our luggage and took it downstairs. Since the Holiday Inn was only two blocks away, I really wanted to just walk. But with four large suitcases and three other bags, it was impossible. So the doorman got me a taxi van and I headed over.

I was able to check in even though the room wasn't ready. I left our bags with the concierge and headed back to the Sesame office. When I got there, it was almost time for lunch. They ordered food for everyone and when we were done eating, they finished the table read. Because it was so nice outside, hot actually, we decided to take the 15 block walk to the hotel. The Holiday Inn was much nicer than the previous hotel. We're not particularly picky when it comes to stuff like that, we just want to be comfortable. We got into the room and everyone crashed. It had been an exhausting 24 plus hours and we were tired. We slept for about 3 hours, had dinner at the hotel restaurant, and then crashed again for the rest of the night. Coy and I had a 7 am pick up the next day for what was to be his first day of shooting.

The next morning, Coy and I were picked up in a passenger van at 7am. They were shooting at an elementary school in Harlem that day. When we arrived the 2nd 2nd AD greeted us and led us into the school cafeteria where they had holding set up. She took our breakfast orders and then took us around and introduced us to everyone. We met the wardrobe and hair/makeup people and then headed to Coy's "dressing room" so that he could change into his wardrobe. When he was done, we walked out to a nice surprise...Bill Berner greeted us. He was the Director of Photography [20]on AWTY and told us that he would be doing the same for this show. Bill's wife Carol was one of the *Electric Company* producers. It was Bill who initiated Coy's involvement with the show. When he learned that they

---

[20] *Director of Photography (Cinematographer)-The person on set who is over the camera and lighting crews. He or she is responsible for the look and feel of each shot and works closely with the director in determining how each scene is lit and shot.*

were looking for a kid to play this new character, he suggested

that they look at Coy.

Next, we went to hair/ makeup. We ate our breakfast after that

and then it was time for him to report to set. I headed to craft

services [21]for coffee and to my surprise, realized that it was the

same company that did crafty on AWTY! It was quickly

becoming clear to me that this world, much like the professional

basketball world, was very small. I would later learn that the

majority of the crew that worked on AWTY was from the New

York area. As the summer went on, we would be reunited with

many of them on this set.

Holding was set up inside the cafeteria but they were actually

shooting outside that day. This particular episode was called

"Wordball Games". The cast were all dressed in athletic attire

and were participating in an athletic competition that was

based on reading and spelling words. Coy had a blast. At one

---

[21] *Craft Services(crafty)-The department on a television or movie set that provides buffet style snacks and drinks for the cast and crew.*

point, it started to rain and production was halted. We all hung out in the cafeteria while waiting it out. While there, the cast started an impromptu freestyle rap session. The funny thing to me was the fact that Coy was right in the middle of all of it. Here he was, his first day on set, working with people who at that point were on their third season of working together, and he was hanging with them like he had known them all his life. He's always been a little social butterfly, but clearly he is most comfortable and happy when he's on a set doing what he loves to do with people who share the same passion.

When the day was over, they put us in a car and we headed back to the hotel. We were set to move into our apartment the next day and we wanted to see what it looked like. The Holiday Inn that we were staying in was on W.57th and it turns out that the apartment was on W.60th, just three blocks away. We called TEC and asked if we could go see it. They called the company they were leasing the apartment from to see if it was ok. They told TEC that no one was in the apartment and they were just waiting for it to be cleaned so it was no problem for us to take a look at it. We took the three block walk over to the apartment

building and got the key from the doorman, who was expecting

us. We took the elevator to the 42nd floor and when we got to

the apartment, the door was partially open. I knocked and

pushed it open a little and to my surprise, there was a man and

woman inside. They had suitcases packed by the door and were

apparently waiting for someone. We introduced ourselves and

told them why we were there. They said that they were leaving

shortly and didn't mind if we looked around.

It was a one bedroom apartment with a small kitchen and one

bathroom. There was a pull out couch in the living room and

two televisions, one in the living room, one in the bedroom. It

was much, much, MUCH smaller than what we were

accustomed to, but it would certainly do. We would only be

there for two months and Coy and I would be on set more than

we would be at the apartment. We left and walked up to Bed,

Bath, and Beyond in Lincoln Square and got some sheets and

pillows. We also picked up a few kitchen utensils but the

majority of what we needed was already at the apartment. We

got back to the hotel, ate dinner, and just relaxed for the rest of the evening.

The next morning, the van showed up to take Coy and I to set. This time we had a different driver who would end up being the person who picked us up every day. His name was Alex Norton and he was one of the PA's on set. Alex is a native New Yorker who was on summer break from film school in Paris. We would get to know him really well over the next couple of months. He was a really cool guy who shared a love of films with me. He and Coy and I would have great conversations about different movies on our trips to set every day.

The set was at the same location that day. Things went pretty much the same way they had gone the day before with the exception of one detail…it…was…HOT!! The heat would become the theme that defined the summer. It was hot that day and as the days went by, it would only get hotter. As I had been with every other thing that Coy had done up to this point, I was nervous when he started working the day before. But just as he had done every other time before, he put me at ease when the cameras started to roll. The kid is a natural and this is what he's supposed to be doing. Watching him work and interact with everyone on that second day, you would've thought that he'd been with them since the beginning.

At some point during the day, we got a little rain again. It wasn't enough to force a break in shooting but some people did break out their parkas and umbrellas. While watching them set up and explain the next shot to Coy, I noticed something interesting. One of the PA's had gotten an umbrella and was standing next to Coy, holding it over him. I immediately thought about that day two years prior, standing in the heat in the middle of June on the set of *Nailed*, explaining to Coy that even though there were people holding an umbrella over Jessica Biel's head, she was no better than him. I remembered telling him that one day, he might be in a position that called for someone to do the same for him, and if/when that time came, to remember this day. When I told him that, I had no idea that this day would come so soon.

When the day was over, we took the train with some of the other actors. Josh Segarra, who plays Hector, is an NYU grad from Orlando. Really cool guy who welcomed Coy and made him feel like a part of the family as soon as he met him. Ricky Smith who plays Keith, is a couple of years older than Coy. He was the youngest cast member before Coy came and soon became like an older brother to him. We all walked to the train station together and actually took the same train to a certain point. Josh lived in our neighborhood so we got off at the same stop, 59th st-Columbus Circle. Coy and I then walked to the hotel. Keisha had everything packed up when we got there. Since we were all there together, we were able to just walk everything over to the apartment. Since January, we had stayed at the Holiday Inn in Stamford, CT for two months, the Four Seasons in Beverly Hills for a week, the Residence Inn in El Segundo for two months, the Crowne Plaza in Hollywood, FL for a week, and with friends and family off and on for a month. . We were excited to finally get in our own place. Even if it was going to just be for a little while.

It's interesting because at the time that all of this was going on, I wasn't really thinking about what we were going through. We were on a quest and it was just about getting to the next place to do the next thing. But now, looking back, we did A LOT during that time. I'm extremely proud of my family. It's not easy to be uprooted and taken out of your comfort zone like that. Especially Coy. He was the one who had to perform in spite of all of that.

28

THE END?

It didn't take long for us to get into a routine. Coy and I would go to set everyday and Keisha and Chayse would hang out in the city. This was the great thing about shooting in NY. There was always something for them to do. Plus, Central Park was literally two blocks away. After the first couple of days of shooting at the elementary school, we started going to what would be the location used the most during filming. Jackie Robinson Park on Bradhurst Ave in Harlem was where most of the filming took place. *The Electric Diner* set is located right across the street. The diner is the place on the show where Hector works and where the Electric Company frequently hangs out. Holding was set up at the *Tabernacle of Deliverance Praise and Worship Canter* a block away on Fredrick Douglass Blvd. It was a wonderful experience, shooting on location in that neighborhood, getting to know the people that lived there.

Our experience with The Electric Company is absolutely one of the best we've had as a family. We got to know a lot of the people involved with the show on a personal level and they are all just wonderful people. Keisha and Chayse would take the train to set a couple of times a week and hang out so they got to know the whole family and basically just took us in. It was a great feeling because we had been out of our comfort zone for so long. They really made us feel welcomed.

Ginger Gonzalez was the second AD. She is the one who creates the call sheets, sets the production schedule, etc. She was like a mother bear to us. ANYTHING we needed, she made sure it got done. We've adopted Ginger into our family. She is just an amazingly nice person. Genuine. Sweet. Caring. The boys love her and so do Keisha and I. She made sure that we got home every day after shooting, was constantly checking on Coy throughout the day to make sure he was ok. During the bed bug epidemic in the city, the apartment we were staying in got infested. When we realized it, I told Ginger. Her reaction, "Oh, we've got to get you out of there. You can't stay there." Her reaction set off a chain of reactions amongst the powers that be. The result, we were back at the Holiday Inn that night and in another apartment on the east side a couple of days later. They even paid to have our clothes cleaned.

Karen Fowler is the magnificent executive producer. She runs the whole shabang. She is the reason that the set has the vibe that it does. It all starts with her. She is an energetic, enthusiastic, smart, and passionate person who absolutely loves what she does and brings a positive, creative energy to the set every day.

Jana Camacho was the 2nd 2nd AD. She would always meet us when we arrived in the morning and direct us to where Coy needed to be. She would take his breakfast order and let us know when it was time to go to set, etc. Not that Coy was privileged. She did the same thing for the entire cast. She was really sweet and adored Coy and Chayse.

I mentioned Bill Berner's wife, Carol earlier. Carol Klein was another producer who worked closely with Karen. She is really sweet and has a humor that you wouldn't think she has.

These are just a few of the people involved with that show that made the experience really special for us. The entire cast- Josh Segarra, Ricky Smith, Dominic Colon, Ashley Morris, William Jackson Harper, Sandie Rosa, Priscilla Diaz, Carly Rose, Sonenclar, Chris Sullivan, Steve Freitas-were all really cool and super talented people and Coy had so much fun working with them. Priscilla "P Star" Diaz is especially talented and she and Coy became really close.

As I said earlier, there were several crew members working on the show who had worked on AWTY. Like us, they were waiting on the decision about whether or not the show was going to get picked up. The plan that I had at the time was that at the end of the TEC run, we would return to Columbia and make plans to move to LA, just like we were planning to do the previous fall. Keisha hadn't burned any bridges with her contact at the wireless company out there and I didn't see any reason why she couldn't apply for and get a job with them. I would get back on the internet and start looking for a job as well. We could stay with her sister in Columbia and be ready to move by the end of the year, if not sooner. Just in time for pilot season in January.

One day during the last week of July, I got a text from Jaime. They too had been waiting on word about the pick up. The text simply said, "Looks like we'll be moving to Connecticut." Even though I hadn't spoken to him in a few days, I knew exactly what he was talking about. *Are We There Yet* had been picked up for 90 episodes. *Wow.* I called him right away to get the news verbally. Keisha and the boys heard my excitement and came running into the bedroom. I shared the news with them and we all started screaming and jumping up and down and running around the room. *Wow.*

Word travels fast in this business. The next day on set, everyone who had been waiting on the news had heard from their own source. We were all excited about it. It was to be a great opportunity for a lot of people for different reasons. For us it meant stability. At least for a little while. It meant that the gamble had paid off. It said to Coy that if you work hard, put God first, and believe in yourself, things that seem impossible are suddenly possible.

The Electric Company wrapped shooting on September 7. It was a bittersweet day on set that last day. We were excited to begin the new chapter in our lives but sad to say goodbye to our *Electric Company* family whom we had grown to love. There was a wrap party the next night and then the day after that, we were on a flight headed back to Columbia. It didn't seem like that long ago that we had arrived. Staying at the Americana that first night. Walking to Times Square for dinner. Now it was over. The great thing about it is that we left the city with much more than what we had arrived with.

The official announcement and subsequent press release about the 90 episode AWTY order had come out on August 16. By the time we got back to Columbia, John had been in touch with us a few times about it. We had to be in Stamford the first week of October. Coy would start school on the 5th, with production of the show scheduled to begin the following week. We had about 3 ½ weeks before it would be time to go. For us, it was basically a vacation. We didn't have anything to do really since we had already moved out of our house. It was our responsibility to find a place to stay in Stamford so we looked at a few places online and set up some appointments for when we got there.

One night when the boys were asleep, Keisha and I were talking about the past year. It's amazing how quickly your life can change. One day, you're on one path, headed in one direction. The next, your life is completely different and you're doing something that you never dreamed of. We sat there thinking about where we had been. Wondering about where we were going. When would the journey end? *Where* would the journey end? Would we ever be able to stop asking ourselves, are we there yet?

On Friday, Oct. 1, I rented a U-Haul truck, drove to the storage facility that held all of our belongings, and loaded up. On Saturday afternoon, Keisha and the boys piled into the Navigator and pulled out of the driveway behind me. We hit I-95 and headed north...again.

EPILOGUE

On March 13, 2011, Coy won the Young Artists Award for Best Performance In A TV Series (Comedy or Drama), *Supporting Young Actor*, for his work on *Are We There Yet?*.

On June 17, 2011, during his 13th birthday party in Columbia, Coy was awarded with a plaque by Mayor Steve Benjamin's wife, DeAndrea Benjamin, proclaiming June 17th to be COY STEWART DAY in Columbia, SC.

On December 15, 2011, shooting wrapped on the 100th episode of *Are We There Yet?*. TBS holds an option to order additional episodes if they so choose.

In January of 2012, Coy and I will head to Los Angeles for pilot season. Keisha and Chayse will stay behind in Columbia while Chayse finishes kindergarten at Lake Carolina Elementary. Our journey began in the summer of 2008. Three years later, we are no closer to knowing where (or when) it will end. It has been a roller coaster ride that none of us expected. Along the way, we have met some wonderful people, been to some wonderful places, and experienced some amazing things. But nothing is more amazing than watching our children grow and chase their dreams. In 2011, Chayse secured representation with agencies in New York and LA and has started the process of auditioning. He says that he "wants to be an actor like Coy."

Supporting our boys' dreams has given Keisha and myself the opportunity to discover new dreams of our own. To date, I have written three feature film screenplays, one for a television drama, and a treatment for a reality show based on our journey. Keisha is currently pursuing a career as a stylist to child entertainers.

If there is anything that I hope you take from our story, it's the realization that dreams do come true. We are all witness to it every day. Every time you watch someone on television or in a movie. Or see a professional athlete on the court or field. Or see a newscaster on the evening news. Every time you read a book or newspaper article. Every time you turn on your MacBook, IPhone, or any other Apple, Inc product. Through everything we see and do in our everyday lives, we are witnessing someone's dream that has come true. Believe in yourself and in your dreams. Have the courage to pursue them and know that the best thing about doing so is not necessarily the dream itself, but the journey that takes you to it.

Finally... parents. I encourage you to support your kids' dreams as much as you can. Show them the love and support they deserve and they just might show you the world.

God Bless.